# ReVivement

*Having a Life After Retirement*

# ReVivement

## Having a Life After Retirement

## An Uplifting
## Interactive Guide to
## Invigorate
## Your Later Years

GLORIA DUNN-VIOLIN

*How to Enjoy Your Life Until You're at Least 100*
*through Emerging Discoveries and Innovations,*
*Current Day Trends and a Life-Planning Guide*

Having a Life Now Publishing

ATTENTION CORPORATIONS, UNIVERSITIES, AND PROFESSIONAL ORGANIZATIONS: Quantity discounts are available on bulk purchases of this book for educational purposes, sales premiums or fund raising. Special books or book excerpts can also be created to fit specific needs. For quantity purchases of this book:

Having a Life Now Publishers
1537 So. Novato Blvd. #947
Novato, CA 94948
Email: gloria@havingalifenow.com
Phone: 415-259-7090

Library of Congress Control Number: 2017901053
Dunn-Violin, Gloria, 1939-
Revivement: Having a Life After Making a Living/Gloria Dunn-Violin.

ISBN 978-0-9660867-0-6
   1. Retirement, 2. Longevity, 3. Purpose, 4. Health, 5. Work

Publisher's Note: This book is intended to provide general information about retirement life planning. Neither the author nor the publisher is engaged in rendering legal, accounting, financial, medical, or psychological services. The author also does not recommend skateboarding. As each situation is unique, questions specific to your particular situation should be addressed to an appropriate professional for proper evaluation and advice. The author and publisher disclaim any liability, loss, or risk that is incurred as a consequence of the use and application of any of the contents of this work.

Cover design: Gloria Dunn-Violin and Trina Swerdlow
Illustrations: Brian Narelle, briannarelle@comcast.net
Interior design: Jim Shubin, bookalchemist.net

This book is introducing you to a new way to experience your life after 50. As you read, please notice that I am using the word *retirement* for the ending of regular work life and *revivement*™ for your second half of life.

# Dedication

*I dedicate this book to my children, Jennifer and Gabrielle (both Baby Boomers), who I love dearly. Their presence in my life, and their love for me throughout our lives together, has been an incredible gift.*

*Through them I also have been blessed with the joy of family. They've brought into my life their wonderful husbands and, between them, seven grandchildren I so enjoy watching as they grow into unique and delightful individuals.*

# Gratitude

Writing a book is a grand undertaking. In my case, it's about the desire to impart information, hope and guidance to you, the reader about fulfilling, enjoying, and making the most of your life now and in your later years. My hope is that you get value from my research, knowledge, experience and writing, and use all that to positively impact your future.

It's been my privilege and joy to develop and write this book, and oversee its design and birth. Yet, without other eyes and ears, it would not have the same quality.

I appreciate the professional guidance with structure, readability, accuracy, design, and creativity, and the support I've had from family and friends. I have several people to acknowledge here for their contributions to the actualization of this book.

My dear husband and love, Donald Violin, who is my co-publisher and behind-the-scenes doer, supporter, cheerleader and best friend. He always stands with me. He believes in me. Can anyone ask for a greater gift?

My dear friend Trina Swerdlow, whose art direction and wordsmith skills took my book cover concept and design to a higher level. Previously a designer, she is now an author (Stress Reduction Journal) and a certified clinical hypnotherapist, who uses her skills and loving heart to help others.

Leslie Keenan, whose expertise as a developmental editor helped me structure my content so that you, the reader, could follow me throughout the book. I appreciate her suggestions for improving my copy as well as her encouragement.

Bobbi Rubenstein, a dear friend and unbelievable editor, who read my copy and made suggestions that have been invaluable. Her skill and honesty are precious.

Bob Stein, my dear friend of many years, who let me know my first draft of the book had potential but was not enough. He took his busy time to read and proof the entire draft, notate his comments, and encourage me to try again. He was right!

Linda Jay, a superb copyeditor, who did a great job in correcting wording and punctuation to give the book its final touches of professionalism.

My good friend Jim Prost, who has coached my speaking skills and helped me develop my Power Point throughout the years. Most currently, I am taking the messages in this book out into the world as a professional speaker with his guidance and visuals.

Brian Narelle, whose talent as an illustrator has given this book delightful visuals for you to enjoy.

Jim Shubin, who created the interior design and my back cover to complete the birthing of this book.

Thank you too, to others who journeyed with me on parts of this book: Gail Haar, Kim Torgerson, Woody Weingarten, and Laurie Nardone.

I also want to thank all of the friends and strangers, who kindly told me their stories. Without them, I wouldn't have the realness that I want this book to share with like-minded travelers on their way to their second half of life.

I also want to acknowledge Bill Vespa and Tracy Rempe at Zenith Printing for their work on designing my promotional art, and their involvement in the final touches on the cover of this book.

I appreciate all the curious, investigative, and brilliant explorers of science, longevity, wellness, and personal growth whose amazing discoveries, wisdom, guidance, and products have gifted us with the potential to have a better life.

Lastly, to all those whose shoulders I stand upon who discovered the importance of life's purpose, spoke and wrote about values, challenged ageism, made us aware of lifestyle choices, taught us about personal growth, researched and discovered new modalities to increase our lifespan, and in so many ways educated us while they turned the world upside down, encouraging us to change for the better.

To All a Heartfelt Thank You!

# Contents

Most of the people in stories in this book are composites of more than one real person. I've changed names, facts, and other identifying words to protect the privacy of those who took their time to share their stories with me. I thank them most appreciatively. Only Ted Robinson's real name is used, and Jack is a made-up character to demonstrate one way to use this book.

Know that my intention is to give you insight into new research, ideas, and lifestyles that will support your revivement. I hope this leading-edge information will delight you as it has fascinated me, and that you will be inspired to continue to explore beyond this book to learn more. Also know I am not a medical practitioner or scientist, and I rely on extensive research to present this information.

I developed the exercises in the back of this book to support you in your revivement journey. You might choose to do them independently or in a Mastermind or Book Study Group, where you can support each other in completing and activating the exercises.

My cover photo is intended to represent my energy and sense of fun, and is a metaphor to underscore the message that you and I have the ability to move forward into our time of revivement together. It is not an invitation to try skateboarding.

# Preface

## My Non-Grata Retirement

The phone rang. "Sorry Gloria, we no longer have a budget for your services. We won't be doing any more projects for a while," said my biggest client. Then, slowly, one client after another called with the same bad news, as the 2008 recession stole the work I had enjoyed doing for 25 years. It tiptoed in and snatched away the very arena in which I had happily used my skills and knowledge. I had given my heart to my work, and these phone calls seemed to erase the possibility of doing what I loved to do as well as eliminate my source of income. Corporate budgets were frozen, and all my clients were gone in one fell swoop. It was like being fired or laid off. Like being given a pink slip on a Friday. Devastating!

Now what? There was an emptiness in my life—a void that I would now need to fill. But how? I wasn't expecting to be forced into an early retirement. In fact, I had no intention of ever retiring. I had never even thought about it.

Now the work I enjoyed and my income were both gone. I was forlorn. I wasn't sure what I was going to do with the rest of my life. Clearly, I had not planned ahead.

By that time, my age was also an issue, and so I figured being without my work was how life was going to be. Society had set me up to think my options were limited as an older person, and that I would be judged by a number—my age. I figured I was lucky to have lasted as long as I did in the business world. With ageism alive and well, I didn't even consider looking for new work. I knew it would be very challenging, and I gave up, making an uneasy, joyless peace with my new existence.

But I'm an active person, and knew that just hanging around home would not be healthy for me. I started to look at what I might do to fill my time. I eventually found several activities that were of interest.

First, I decided to volunteer. I joined a Rotary Club, where "service above self" is the motto. And, since I always felt my work was to be of service by helping people live their best work life possible, Rotary seemed like a good fit.

It gave me the opportunity to give and do good while using my inherent and trained skills. I've always said I can be a leader, a team player, or a follower. At Rotary, I was able to be all three.

Also, I took some great classes at Olli, Osher Lifelong Learning Institute, a university program for adults over 55. The Osher Foundation supports 119 lifelong learning programs on university and college campuses across the country. It has at least one grantee in each of the 50 states and the District of Columbia. You might have one in your area. Check their national website. Look for the List of Institutes at: http://www.osherfoundation.org.

I also took an acting class at the community college. I already had been on stage as a speaker. Now, I wanted to explore getting on the stage as an actress.

Even with all these outlets, I really missed my work as a workshop leader, consultant, coach, and speaker. So, I got a part-time job as a Weight Watchers Leader. Again, I could help others with something I understood, the challenges of losing weight. That was fun for a while, and I was able to use my skills. In fact, I thought I had come full circle, because I had been a Weight Watchers Leader in my late 20's. But after two years, it wasn't enough. I felt I had something more I wanted to do, but I didn't know what, or how to find it. I continued my search. What I found was good, but not soul-grabbing.

Then, about six years after I thought my work life was over, I found the answer to my next career. I read an article in the newspaper about a retirement life coach and thought, "I can do that!" After all, I have 25 years of experience in organizational development training and coaching employees, so I know how to help people achieve their personal and work goals. My first career of ten years included two years as a consultant and eight as a manager of public relations departments; so again, I understand people issues and was able to mentor those on my staff to succeed. Plus, since I lost my business I know how it feels to be retired, and the confusion and emptiness it can bring into one's life. I guess you could say this all was training me for my future—for the career I have today.

After my "aha" moment, realizing there was a new direction, a new career for me, I immediately took a retirement coach certification course and started putting my talks and materials together. I got on the phone and called people I knew, as well as service organizations, and booked 32 speaking engagements. The talks I gave were great, because the feedback I got from my audiences let me know I was on the right path. I continue to give speeches today because I want to continue to help others see how to have a vital life after retirement.

As my spirit led me, I got back into my role as educator, cheerleader, and supporter, bringing emerging information about post-retirement life with its problems and solutions out into the public. I began to write a monthly article for a local newspaper and a blog for my website, and I started writing this book.

I was using myself and my own experiences and feelings. This quote by George Bernard Shaw is relevant to me:

*"I want to be thoroughly used up when I die, for the harder I work the more I live. I rejoice in life for its own sake. Life is no 'brief candle' for me. It is a sort of splendid torch which I have got hold of for the moment, and I want to make it burn as brightly as possible before handing it on to future generations."*

Not only did I have to handle the loss of my work, but also I needed to deal with the misconceptions around age. If someone hears a number—your age—they put you in a box. You are categorized as an old fogie. But you don't have to accept that stereotype.

Sure, my body may have some challenges. But, my mind and spirit, my skills and capabilities, my competence and good work ethic are alive and well. I'm ready to roll. Yes, I'm what you call "retirement age," or even past it. But as you will learn in reading this book, I don't have a retiring personality. I have a get-up-and-go-and-do personality. Discovering what I'm going to get up and go and do is a never-ending quest for me, one that has taken me down roads I never dreamed of as a child or a young adult, and one that's given me enormous joy.

In fact, when I spoke to a group recently, I was ready to do the Big Reveal. I was going to come out of the closet about my age. Of course, because my birthday had just passed, someone beat me to it and put on Facebook that I had just turned 77. What I told the group was that just because the earth had traveled around the sun 77 times since I've been on this planet doesn't make me old.

I also told the audience that I don't plan to retire. Ever! I'm pursuing my purpose. I'm passionate about what I'm doing. I'm using my skills and myself. And I pray I'm helping people. That's my bottom line. Why would I give up that possibility just because somebody else defines me by a number?

I figured if I'm lucky, I have at least another 25 years to live, learn, laugh, and love. I'm not one to sit around. In fact, this riles me so that I'm out to bust ageism no matter what a person's age is. Whether younger or older, each person has something to contribute, and each of us can help others achieve new vistas of growth and becoming.

I have found my purpose, and today I'm guiding people on how to have a good life both before and after retirement. I'm helping them understand that older isn't over, it's better. It's what gets me up in the morning and I'm having a blast. And, again, I'm having a fulfilling life.

*I BELIEVE*

*I believe we become who we are by being aware,*
*handling life's challenges, and moving on.*

*I believe we have the capacity to do so much more*
*than we allow ourselves to do.*

*I believe we become who we are when we honor our*
*gifts and skills and use them to help others.*

*I believe that helping others helps us.*

*And, I believe that the best time of life is now.*

— Gloria Dunn-Violin

{Please note that I use a prototype, Jack, in the story below. Jack demonstrates how someone can find the support and answers he or she needs by reading the next few pages. With my desire to give you insight on how you might want to use this book, I took creative license in writing it as a story as if Jack already had gone through the information and worksheets.}

## A Happy Beginning: How Jack Used This Book

Jack wakes up on his first day of revivement and knows that today is going to be the start of an exciting adventure. Perhaps even the beginning of the best time of his life.

He's been waiting for this for a long time—33 years, to be exact. He has worked hard, long hours all these years and been a responsible man, supporting his family and serving his company. But now, it's his turn. It's time to do all the things he has in his plan.

When Jack picked up my book six months before he retired, he decided he would follow my instructions to read the book and then develop his revivement plan. He allowed the book's guidance to prepare him for his future.

Jack first read about the pleasant possibilities as well as the pitfalls of what his second half of life could be. The choices were to do nothing, get sick, or get depressed. Or do what the book advised and have a great life. No contest there. He made the better choice.

"Chapter two," he said, "told me about some fascinating discoveries about the brain and body that I didn't know. I had been too busy with my job to pay attention to what I thought were not important matters. Boy, was I wrong. This stuff is fascinating. I learned I can keep my brain smarter and younger if I do brain exercises. I knew about exercising to keep my body healthy, but I had never looked at the whole picture of health before. I learned how technology is being used to aid the older generation. I also learned about longevity and how scientists are making so many discoveries for our benefit."

As he read, Jack began to identify his fears and concerns about getting older. All the euphemisms about older people and their circumscribed lives came to mind. He shuddered. He certainly didn't want that for himself. But as he read the stories in the book about active, energetic people in their 60's, 70's, 80's, and 90's, he relaxed. He realized that if they could do what they are doing at their age—after all he is only approaching 65—he could do even better.

"Then I read about dealing with change and loss. I don't like change, but I have adapted to new circumstances over the years. It was comforting to see there is a process I can use to help me adjust emotionally to my transition.

"Another chapter about planning the rest of my life gave me a good overview of how revivement affects different people and how to start thinking of what my future will be like. It helped me see a bigger picture.

"I started feeling positive about my impending revivement. Like Gloria said, I don't need to wait until I retire. So I decided to start adding new ideas from the book into my life right away.

"As I went through the book, I got to the information about personal purpose. Never thought about that before. I, probably like a lot of people, had just worked to make a paycheck. Now, Gloria is telling me that if I find my personal

23

purpose, I will know what the rest of my life is about. Hard to believe, but I'm willing to give it a try."

The following chapters took Jack through other aspects of life that would give him balance. Chapters on Relationships, Ongoing Learning, Health/Wellness, Volunteerism, Spirit, Leisure, and more. "At the end of the book, I read about leaving a legacy," said Jack. "Again, this is something I had never thought about before. Now I realized that I want to leave a legacy for my family and the world."

Once Jack finished reading all the chapters, he started using the activity sheets in the back of the book. In one exercise, he saw his history of accomplishments, ups and downs, family of origin and how he grew as a person. The awareness was inspiring.

By filling in another activity sheet, he realized that he had inherent talents and over the years had acquired many skills. Jack also had a lot of world and work experience. He felt good about himself after he saw himself in this new way. He had never stopped to analyze his assets and how he might use them.

"In each case, as I filled out the worksheets," said Jack, "I liked knowing I could adjust them if I changed my mind. I like flexibility, so that helped," he added.

Another activity sheet had Jack list his knowledge, preferences, desires, hobbies, and more. He realized he had a wealth of experience to bring to his new adventures. "Wow, he thought. I didn't realize I was that good," he said as he chuckled at his bravado in addressing his qualities.

"I used the worksheets to begin defining my purpose. It took concentration and focus. I filled in the forms and began to see a new me emerge. I took Gloria's advice to take time to think about what I've written down and be willing to redo the worksheet until it feels right. Once I thought I had it, the next step was to put it into a mission statement. I always thought mission statements were only for businesses. I learned I can have one for my life and that by having a mission statement, I'll be giving myself a guide for how to direct my energy."

"The last two exercises are a wrap-up of my entire plan, incorporating all my worksheets into my personal guide. I read it, made adjustments confirming my proposed actions, and gave it a timeline. Now I was ready to enjoy the rest of my life.

I have been retired for a year and started using the book 18 months ago. The book was a great guide. Many things I planned have fallen into place. With a few adjustments, I've been enjoying this stage of my life."

"I was glad that one of the exercises gave me the option to take a breather the first six months of my revivement if I wanted to by guiding me to think about how I wanted to spend those days," said Jack. Later in the book, you'll see how he chose to use his first six months.

# *Introduction*

*"The afternoon knows what the morning never suspected."*
— ROBERT FROST, Author and Poet

You and I are alive at an amazing time in the history of the human race. Never before has a generation as a whole been graced with the potential of living another 30, 40, 50 or more years—a future where millions of people have the potential to become centenarians. Never before did we get to retire to a second half of life that promised to reward the fruits of our labor with fulfillment and joy. Never before did we have a futurist's view of our extended tomorrow graced with new discoveries, inventions, and life-saving miracles. We have the gifts of healthy longevity, freedom to be who we are and do what we want, and awareness that will extend our personal potential beyond previous limitations.

As you climb toward our wisdom years after the age of 50, you can use many of today's innovations to seek a new way to live, and create the best life possible. After all, you've earned it. Your previous years filled you with experience, knowledge, skills, interests, and so much more. Now you get to take it all into your glorious future.

Today, as an older adult, you are more fortunate than ever before. You will benefit from many new scientific, health-related and technological discoveries on your trip to your personal tomorrow. Those who came before us didn't have these options. But, today you can revise old ideas with updated research, and expand the possibilities before you.

Welcome to the 21st century and your second half of life. I'm excited to share with you some of these new life-giving gifts that are going to give you a great future no matter your age. In fact, you may think you've found the Fountain of Youth. After all, as you will learn, you have the privilege of drinking or bathing in the waters of the latest discoveries. If you embrace these gifts, you might just become a little younger. I'm also going to give you some building blocks on which to strengthen the foundation of your new future, and tell you why the old idea of retirement needs to be replaced with words like renewal, reinvention, and rebirth. And, I've created a new word to express and replace the word retirement. I'm calling this precious time of life *revivement*.

With a desire to change the old concept of retiring, which means over and done, to a new and fulfilling concept, I will use the word revivement in this book when I talk about the present and future. I will use the word retirement when I talk about old thinking and the past. Perhaps, together, we will begin to use revivement to redesign our futures as we revive ourselves and move forward.

Additionally, I will share with you what I've learned about revivement and aging, and how both areas challenge us in today's society. Yet both make our bonus years possible. But, first, let's explore a little history of how you came to be the way you are today.

## Baby Boomers Changed the World

If you're a baby boomer, born between 1946 and 1964, you changed everything. Your contributions to the world are Herculean. As you aged into your late teens and early 20s, you provoked the world with challenges that helped us grow as individuals and as a society. You continue to take getting older head-on, leading the way today, as another baby boomer turns 65 every eight seconds. Ten thousand of you a day will become 70 million over the age of 65 by 2030.

You are changing the face of retirement to revivement as you adopt new lifestyles that your parents never had the chance to enjoy.

Do you remember rebelling against your parents and society with your music? Do you remember how John Lennon described your optimistic thinking? He sang, "You may say that I'm a dreamer. But I'm not the only one. I hope someday you'll join us. And the world will be as one."

You witnessed and participated in some of the greatest social changes in the country's history. It was you in the 1960s who marched alongside Rev. Martin Luther King, Jr. in the American civil rights movement. It was you who became feminists along with Gloria Steinem and Betty Friedan, bringing women's rights front and center. Can you imagine your parents doing those things?

A new social conscience rose among you as young citizens, and you fought for social, economic, and political equality and justice for many disadvantaged groups. Without you, many of today's laws that protect these diverse groups might not exist.

Young women began to work in male-dominated professions. You coined terms such as the "glass ceiling" and the "equal opportunity workplace." You started using personal style training programs at your companies to develop awareness of how to get along with all co-workers.

From how you performed business to new inventions to even forcing a change in the Constitution, baby boomers ruled. Because of your push to lower the voting age, Congress passed the 26th Amendment in March 1971, allowing young people between 18 and 21 to vote.

Thousands of useful, productive, and life-changing inventions came from the masterful minds of baby boomers. Miraculous innovations like computers, the web, and the cell phone increased our personal freedoms in the following decades. They transformed our jobs and personal lives for good. Millions of products and services we take for granted today did not exist before you, the baby boomers, entered the world.

You can be just as innovative by inventing the next stages of your life. By adopting the new thinking in this book, you'll be able to transform the old into the new and ease into your later years without struggle. If you are willing to use the information in these chapters to revise some of your thoughts, practices, and expectations, you will change old ways and embrace a new way of living.

I also hope to inspire those of you who love their work to keep working, but on your own terms. I want to bust the idea of your age being a definitive end point to any part of life.

This book will enlighten you. It will describe the new research to help your brain become smarter and younger, increasing your memory, and influencing your genes, as well as the physical and mental advances that support your health and wellness. I'll also talk about the beauty of age and its gifts, and guide you into areas of personal growth. Then I'll cover the nine pillars to making your life whole, meaningful and happy.

The last section of the book is a planning guide and workbook with activity sheets that will help you create the future you want. It will even walk with you through your first six months of revivement and support you through your later years based on who you are, what you need, and what you want to do. This guide will be your best friend, supporting you as you take each step to actualize the future you want. Use it and enjoy the benefits of more certainty as you accomplish each step in your journey.

# Chapter
# One

*Age is Beautiful*

*"There is a fountain of youth: it is your mind, your talents,
the creativity you bring to your life and the lives of people you love.
When you learn to tap this source,
you will truly have defeated age."*

— SOPHIA LOREN, Actress

## On Top of the Hill

Many will say that after the age of 50 you are going downhill.
I argue with that. Climbing the mountain of life is a
continuous journey laced with gifts that bring us the personal
wholeness we work so hard to achieve. I prefer to think that
we are always on top of one hill and climbing up the next to
untold rewards.

What do you do when they say you're over the hill, but you're
really on top of it? You say, "WOW, look at me! Do you
realize the thousands of hours I've put in to becoming me?"
482,130 hours at age 55. 569,790 hours at age 65. 657,450
hours at age 75. Then you say, "Do you know all the things
I've learned, seen, experienced?" You add, "Have you any idea
how my life journey and yours intersect? I can do more with
who I am now than who I was then."

Just think about all that you've accomplished in life—from getting up in the morning to face an uncertain day to overcoming the many obstacles that have been placed in your path. These teachers (obstacles) have made you strong, resilient, smart, skilled, and so much more. So, as you show why you are on top of the hill, you produce a few examples. They usually come out in the form of stories, which people love to hear. They are your stories—the building blocks of your life. They made you who you are because you learned from them.

Then you say, "As I look across the breadth of my life, I marvel at the fact that I'm still here, still excited, and doing amazing things." Then you tell them about all you've accomplished in life and make them smile. Why? Because if they are young, they will have something to look forward to. And, if they are your age, they will see that they have something to get excited about.

When we were younger, we didn't have all of the knowledge, experience, and skills we have now. We engaged in life to gain these qualities. We looked at our lives, made changes and took risks. We still need to do that, but now we can make adjustments at a higher level of understanding and purpose.

One expert summarizes beautifully how our essence trumps our chronological and physical age. "Among other things, our bodies no longer respond with the same speed, strength, and grace they once did. But, our internal resources are not gone; they are just rearranged. Where there was strength, determination now appears. Where speed once carried the day, now thoughtful understanding wins it. Where once sensory sharpness gave us an edge, now patience and wisdom provide us with sustaining power," writes Dr. Richard Johnson, author of The New Retirement: Discovering Your Dream.

*"If I can challenge old ideas about aging, I will feel more
and more invigorated. I want to represent this new way.
I want to be a new version of the 70-year-old woman.
Vital, strong, very physical, very agile.
I think that the older I get, the more yoga I'm going to do."*

— JAMIE LEE CURTIS, ACTRESS

Age is a mystery. It's a mix of attitude and genes, childhood
and adult development, awareness and action. It is an inward
journey manifesting itself in how we live our lives inside
and out.

Age shows up as maturity that we turn into wisdom. Our
spirit emanates from within us and fills our goodness with joy
and giving. The physical body keeps our treasures in motion
as it displays the external weathering of time. Age is
beautiful, because with age we are so much more.

What is unique about being over 50 that gives us top-of-the-hill status:

- Experience—Been there, done that
- Wisdom—Acquired from trial and error and stored for the benefit of ourselves and others
- Skills—Proof positive that we know what we're doing
- Intuition—Proven time after time to be right
- Attitude—"My way or the highway" doesn't exist anymore. We've learned how to get along and build relationships
- Perseverance—We've gone through the fire, and came out stronger, more resilient, and better equipped to handle life
- Energy and Enthusiasm—Our internal drive that got us to where we are today
- Realness—What you see is what you get, and it's good
- Accomplishment—Able to use our skills to be productive and succeed
- Humility—Understanding the value of our lives, and grateful for the gifts
- Contribution—Giving back through volunteerism and support of others

What is your attitude about your age? What do you think makes you seem young or old? How do you view people of different ages?

### Ted

*I saw Ted Robinson, who was 95, give a talk about his adventures in World War II and his relationship with then-Navy officer John F. Kennedy. His audience was a mix of age groups.*

*Ted spoke with vitality, humor, and clear-headedness. His voice was strong, his thinking logical, and his stories funny. He stayed on his feet the entire 45 minutes.*

*He may look old, but that's just his outside shell. Inside of him is a volcano of energy that wants to come out and play. He has written books and given speeches, and to this day continues to run his speaking business.*

*What causes someone like him to keep going? The answer is strong purpose backed by powerful skills that he has honed throughout his lifetime. He has determination and will, and perhaps good genes. Most importantly, he has something to look forward to every day that uses who he is in the best way possible.*

Born in 1919, Ted kept an audience of all ages mesmerized for 45 minutes.

Age is based on the number of rotations the earth takes around the sun. You can accept that for your physical age on earth. But, if you are trying to figure out another way to decipher how old you really are, you could use data from the Pew Research Center's survey. The survey says the older people become, the younger they feel. The Center surveyed 3,000 adults 18 and older, and found some startling statistics.

Most adults over age 50 felt at least 10 years younger than their actual age. Among those ages 65 to 74, one-third said they felt 10 to 19 years younger, and one-sixth of those 75 and older said they felt 20 years younger. Of course, there are the young-olds and the old-olds in every age category. There are some 30-year-olds who seem old, and some 95-year-olds who seem young.

According to research sociologist Bernice Neugarten, the young-old represent the majority of older adults. They remain vigorous and are healthy, competent, engaged in activities and satisfied with their role in society. The old-old are individuals who are frail, suffer from poor health and need medical attention, care or support. In general, those who are 85-plus have been considered the old-old. But that definition is changing, too. Just consider 95-year-old Ted or my 96-year-old friend, Ellie.

## Ellie

*Ellie is alert and sharp. She can remember events that happened decades ago as well as recently. She remembers our last phone call, even though it might have been a few months ago. Ellie is well read, knows what's going on in the world, and has her own opinions.*

*Ten years ago Ellie lost her husband, who was her teammate, best friend, and life partner for 62 years, and she had to adjust to living on her own. Although her children and grandchildren visit her and stay in touch, she knows that her life is her responsibility. Early on she established a schedule to keep herself active. She is a member of AAUW (American Association of University Women), volunteers at a museum, serves on several committees, and continues to get involved in new activities.*

*When I know I'm going to be in her neighborhood, I call to see if she will be available for a visit. I love it when she tells me, "Oh honey, I'm so sorry, but I'm busy. I'm a docent at the museum today at that time." Of course, we find other times to get together.*

## The Gifts of Age

Age may be in the body, but youth lives in the mind. The fountain of youth lies beneath your skin, lives between your bones, jumps around in your brain, and moves with lightning speed when you keep your interests, spirit, joyfulness, and a positive attitude self-fueled and potent. That kind of energy doesn't want to retire. It wants to live a whole life that includes the riches available to all of us in our hearts, minds, and souls. We just need to reach out.

In contrast, ageism is not good for anyone. As baby boomers, we have an opportunity to lead the way toward a new perspective on getting older. We need to teach the world we will not succumb to a degrading definition of age. Actually, people of any age, including teenagers, react to society's misplaced judgment of them as a group or individuals. Denigrate them, and they suffer from low self-esteem, misinformed that they have no value, which affects their lives and their participation in the world.

Harmful words and implications damage us emotionally and physically. "Negative stereotypes are hurtful to older people, and may also shorten their lives," finds psychologist Becca Levy, PhD, assistant professor of public health at Yale University in an article in the Journal of Personality and Social Psychology. In Levy's study of 660 people 50 years and older, those with more positive self-perceptions of aging lived 7.5 years longer than those with negative self-perceptions of aging.

People's positive beliefs and attitudes boost their mental health. Levy has found that older adults exposed to positive environments have significantly better memory and life balance, whereas negative self-perceptions contribute to diminished memory and feelings of worthlessness.

*I am not a has-been. I am a will be.*
—Lauren Bacall, *Actress*

If we do away with others' concepts of "old age," then what is "retirement age?" I strongly argue against using the phrase; it's stereotypical. There is no age that dictates we must stop living a full and fulfilling life. Instead, we need to reinvent how and what we want to do, as we always have. For example, forty-year-olds are not doing the same things in the same ways they were doing them when they were 30. And for most of us who are many decades older, we're not doing the same things in the same way, either. We grow! We emerge! We become!

I am convinced that the gifts of age can be gratifying for many of us. No matter where we are in life, we can move to a higher level based on how we think and feel. Think of freedom and self-acceptance mixed with wisdom. You don't have to be as unsure, unknowing, or unassuming as you were when you were young and figuring out life. You can boldly show up as an intelligent and creative you with knowledge and high self-regard. Don't we wish we had felt that freedom at a much younger age? At least we can appreciate that we feel it now.

And, we continue to evolve. We've learned so many lessons during our lifetimes. Some through the school of hard knocks, some through patient parents and mentors, and some just because we were in the right place at the wrong time. Yes, those wrong times were good teachers, weren't they?

When Gloria Steinem turned fifty, she described her first 50 years as "leaving a much-loved and familiar country," and turning 60 as arriving at the border of a new country in which she looked forward to "trading moderation for excess, defiance for openness, and planning for the unknown." Today, at 82, Gloria Steinem is vibrant and still impacting younger generations with truths and dares. Years ago, we were amazed when Grandma Moses began painting in her 70s. Today, 70 is at least the new 55, and we aren't surprised anymore. We see people embrace the second half of life with gusto and do things of which they never dreamed.

How do we make age our friend? How do we accept where we are in life and honor our existence? First, we need to think young. Our essence is alive and well. When it comes to age, you might prefer to set yours based on Bernard Baruch's adage, "To me old age is always 15 years older than I am."

Youth lives in your brain when you think young. Yes, your physical body may be having challenges. After all, you've been using it a long time. But your essence has been getting stronger and more adaptable. It's been getting wiser and worldlier. And by now, let us hope, you know yourself.

What makes you laugh? What touches your heart and makes you tear up? How do you respond to others? Do you smile? Do you show your stuff? What is your stuff? Is it how to solve a problem, or design a room, or get up and speak like Ted Robinson? What's your uniqueness? What are your gifts?

Just think of what happens to you when you get excited about something. The anticipation, the possibilities, the happening itself—don't they uplift you? Don't you feel a whole lot better than when you are sitting at home watching TV all day? I say you have every reason to feel better. And I say that when you are out and about, you have every reason to stand tall and be proud that you've reached an age that few prior generations were privileged to achieve.

It's hard to believe that at one time, adults only lived to the age of 30, then 40, then 50. Lifestyle and medical care advances brought us to today, where many of us might live to become centenarians.

Because of people like us, there is a major shift in the concept of revivement in the 21st century, upgrading the old retirement model to an exciting new way to live. Today it is possible to look at our second half of life as a new beginning: taking all of the smarts we've acquired to where we are now and using them to heighten the joy in the rest of our years.

### Revivement—Change the Word and Change Your World

The idea of retirement is now being redesigned because we are living longer, and a new revivement paradigm has emerged. If you are the current revivement age, you might have 30 or 40 more years to do whatever you want. You're not going to want to waste that time sitting on a porch somewhere in your rocking chair. There is another reason you don't want to sit on the porch. According to numerous studies on aging, people who have no plan for their lives after retirement sometimes get depressed. Or, they get sick. Or, they die. You don't want that. So, what do you want?

## *John*

*You don't want to mimic John. He couldn't wait to retire. John had been giving 110% at his job for 33 years. He lived, slept, and ate through his work as an executive director of marketing for a top computer firm. Although he liked his job, he still fantasized about retirement, when he could relax. It was the carrot on a stick just beyond his reach that kept him working hard until the day he would receive his gold watch, goodbye party and retirement package.*

*He told me that when he retired he would no longer have to attend meetings, facilitate employee disputes, or write reports. He was going to be able do whatever he wanted to. In fact, he wouldn't have to get out of bed if he didn't want to. He could just hang out in his favorite chair and read all day or watch television. You get the picture. Whew! His time!*

*Only thing is John never stopped to think, or better yet, plan what his time was really going to look like.*

*The first few weeks of his retirement went by as John sat around reading the newspaper, having that second cup of coffee, playing a little golf. But, that was starting to get old. "Now what?" Now we're a few months into retirement, and little by little John is getting bored. Same thing, day in and day out. He is not happy. Something is missing.*

*Negative ideas began to form in his mind. He realizes he's not sure who he is any more. He couldn't call himself an executive director of marketing or say he worked for a big company. How would he describe himself? Who was he? He felt like a nobody. His persona was disappearing. He also started missing his coworkers, even the ones he complained about. At least they added spice to his day.*

*He and his wife did travel a little, and they visited the grandkids once in a while. But something important inside of John was missing, and he didn't know what it was. You see, when he retired, he had the old definition of retirement in mind.*

It looks like this. Retirement is an ending. Life is over. You are relieved from working, thinking, schedules, and all the other things you've been complaining about for your entire work life. You don't have to do a thing except exist. Oh! Oh! That doesn't sound good!

Many retirees pass away six months to two years after retirement. Scientists posit that the loss of their schedule, structure, sense of community with coworkers, and lack of purpose to direct their energies meant they no longer knew what they would do with each day. The meaning they found in their work was gone. These are vital areas that keep us engaged in our daily pursuits. They keep us alive.

At work, people know what they are going to do every day from 9 to 5, 40 or more hours a week. Then they know what their weekends are going to be like—getting over the 40 hours a week by having fun. Of course, there is a vacation or two, and holidays.

So now they are home, their time is open-ended, and they don't know what to do with their time or themselves. Some try idle busyness, finding things to fill up what threatens to be an empty day. But those things are not necessarily satisfying. With few satisfying outlets they soon become depressed.

Don't you agree that someone in this state needs to acquire new thinking, and go out and discover a new way to live?

A May 2013 report published by the London-based Institute of Economic Affairs found that retirement increased the chances of suffering from depression by 40%, while it increased the probability of having at least one diagnosed physical ailment by about 60%. The report indicated that the impact was assessed after controlling for the usual age-related conditions.

These changes may be why retirement is ranked 10th on the list of life's 43 most stressful events. Some people smoothly make the transition into a successful revivement. Others don't.

## Samantha

*Samantha, a single woman, told me that when she stumbled out of bed one morning after being retired for two weeks, she looked at the clock and thought, "What am I up to today?" She drew out her iPhone and checked her calendar. "First the coffee—can't do a thing without at least one cup. Okay, let's look! Haircut at 10 am; dinner with friends at 6 pm. Nothing in the middle? Oh, no! Now what?"*

*When she worked full-time and often put in extra hours, she had ached for days like this. She hungered for a time when she would not have to meet anyone else's expectations and just could do her own thing. But right now she doesn't know what that is. Her day looks like a void. That's not so bad for just one day or even two, but this is day number 89 since she retired. This isn't going well!*

*Samantha had retired just past her 65th birthday. She was programmed to think that the next life step was retirement, but she never thought what that meant. More importantly, she hadn't considered what her life was going to look like for another 30 or more years. She hadn't taken the time to project herself into the future and develop her next phase. Like most people who retire, Samantha woke up to find nothingness in her life.*

People like Samantha and John need to understand revivement and how to begin the new life that awaits them.

## Health Issues

Gabriel Sahlgren, director of research at the Centre for Market Reform of Education, was surprised by just how much retirement undermined health. He studied 9,000 people in 11 European Union countries and found that across borders, people suffered in the same way... two to three years into retirement, retirees' mental and physical conditions began deteriorating.

Between 1992 and 2005, Dhaval Dave, an associate professor of economics at Bentley University in Waltham, Massachusetts, studied 12,000 Americans and found that, on average, people experience some sort of ailment within six years of retiring. "Hypertension, heart disease, stroke and arthritis are common physical ailments," Dave said. He also found that depression increased after retirement.

A new salvo comes from researchers at the Harvard School of Public Health. They looked at rates of heart attack and stroke among men and women in the ongoing U.S. Health and Retirement Study. Among 5,422 individuals in the study, those who had retired were 40% more likely to have had a heart attack or stroke than those who were still working. The increase was more pronounced during the first year after retirement, and leveled off after that.

## Sad Stories

Whenever I give my speeches and workshops, people stay after the program to share their sadness with me about family, friends and coworkers who were not prepared to retire. The results were often depression, illness, and death. Here are but a few of the many stories I've heard.

A young woman came up to me after one of my talks and said, "My grandmother worked until she was 75. But they pushed her out because of her age, and she died before she was 76."

A gentleman who introduced me at a speaking engagement spoke of his grandfather, who had always been successful. He purchased a house in a new city and kept the old one, thinking he'd have two options for where to spend his reviving days. Unfortunately, the stress of retiring plus handling the move was so great, he died of a heart attack prior to moving. He was only in his mid 60s. He had made a cursory retirement plan without taking into account what that plan actually entailed.

Some people decide their own fate.

*One man described his friend, Dom, who had worked with him for years. "He was a quiet guy, a nice guy, and a hard worker," I was told. He also hardly drank when the guys went out after work Friday nights. But, once Dom retired, he hung around his house doing nothing but watching television. His wife tried to get him to go out into the world, but he thought she was just nagging. His friend invited him to join some activities he was enjoying as a new retiree, but that didn't work, either. Unfortunately, something new and troubling entered the scene, a bottle of scotch. Dom began drinking, and soon drank himself to death.*

The prospect of post-retirement dislocation can even happen to Presidents.

*President Theodore Roosevelt bought into the old definition of retirement. As President he had strong purpose. He was energetic and alive and enacted great reforms for the United States. Then he "retired" from his Presidency too early, and all of a sudden he was lost and became depressed. When he tried to make a comeback, he revitalized his sense of purpose and his sense of self, and the old TR was back on the backs of trains and in front of assemblies making his case to come back and work for his country again. Losing his second bid for the presidency left him with no purpose and no structure, and he fell into a deep depression. Here was a man with so much to give—but he was lost.*

Teddy Roosevelt once said: "The best prize that life has to offer is the chance to work hard at work worth doing." Recent research suggests he may have been more right than he knew. Purposeful work often extends life.

His life continued downhill after all his efforts and interest to re-enter public service were denied. This dedicated conservationist and the man who spearheaded the construction of the Panama Canal, this Nobel Peace Prize winner—for his negotiations to end the Russo-Japanese War—died an unhappy man at the young age of 61.

My impetus for writing this book is to encourage you to take the important steps that I outline so you will have the best second half of life possible. I hope to encourage you to find your passions, follow your dreams, do what you're meant to do, and enjoy your life. So let's get started.

## Taking Charge and Enjoying Revivement

Baby boomers are redefining what retirement is like in the 21st century. You can upgrade the old model to revivement— an exciting new way to live. Today we can look at our second half of life as a new beginning. By using all of the smarts we've acquired to get where we are now, we can heighten the joy for the rest of our lives.

The experiences we've garnered over a lifetime, and the smarts that accompany them give us an advantage we didn't gave in our 20s, 30s, or 40s. You now have the opportunity to renew old passions (activities you always wanted to do but never took the time for), enrich your life, continue growing your sense of self, and so much more. It is a new beginning that can joyfully fill up many years to come.

You get to design your next adventure. No matter your circumstances, there is always a higher road to travel. For some of us, it may be more difficult, but extending yourself to reach it brings untold personal pride. I do think this puts us on the top of the hill.

What did it take to get you where you are—pain, anxiety, sleepless nights? Yes, some of that. Also, willingness to look at our lives and make changes, take risks, and go for what we wanted. We needed people stimulation, activity, interest, passion, and community. Throughout our lives, we've needed to rethink, refocus, and redefine ourselves. And now, at the apex of our lives, we need to find new ways to enjoy today and tomorrow.

But, what does someone who has earnestly kept his or her nose to the grindstone for most of his or her life do to make the shift from work to revivement? How do they go through a big change like this? Well, it's easier than it seems, as you'll find when you do the exercises in the back of this book.

With willingness to go in a new direction, with enthusiasm for finding new ways to enjoy life, and with new tools to get you there, you can do it.

Do you remember when you were a kid? All you knew was what you knew at the time. You didn't yet have the worldly wisdom that you've acquired over your lifetime. You did your best with what you knew, and worked yourself through your decades. But, here you are. You are older, wiser, and more experienced. Wow! Just think what you can do with all of that knowledge.

Where you were to where you are—how you evolved. One door closes, another door opens. Gratefully!

So you've been graced with a long life. What do you want to do with it? There are so many choices. And, you get to choose.

Let's start by giving you information about some exciting discoveries that give you reason to look forward to your future. Let's call them the building blocks to a long and healthy second half of life. Let's measure healthy life by what's possible, understanding that some of us have had or have illnesses that can undermine us if we let them. Instead, we can move forward with what we are able to do. Regardless of our health, we can reprogram our minds to help us live rich, full lives.

We'll also talk about age, because we not only need to change society's perceptions, but our own. After all, age may be in the body, but in my opinion, as I wrote earlier, youth lives in the mind. The fountain of youth lies beneath your skin, lives between your bones, jumps around in your brain, and moves with lightning speed when you keep your interests, spirit, joyfulness, and positive self fueled and potent. That kind of energy doesn't want to retire. It wants to live a whole life that includes the riches available to all of us in our hearts, minds, and souls.

## Jeanie

*Jeanie worked as a reporter, bureau chief, and columnist at the local town newspaper her entire career. "I had no desire or reason to retire. But after I turned 60, I started telling my boss, 'If you think I should retire, I will without objection.' Every year my boss said, 'stay.' I was so glad. I loved my work."*

*Jeanie finally did retire after she remarried at the age of 83. Her boss at the newspaper asked if she would at least continue her column, which she writes to this day at the age of 90. Jeanie said, "I agree with Eleanor Roosevelt, who said she didn't want any life where she wasn't of use."*

*Jeanie has always been a world traveler. Her new husband shares this love, and in their short time together they have traveled across the United States as well as around the world. "When we travel," she said, "we learn so much that is validating about other people and their cultures, and our journeys teach us about things we'd never know if we stayed at home."*

*Jeanie believes everyone needs to be open to new people and opportunities, look for ways to be useful, and have a sense of humor about life and keep laughing.*

# Chapter
# Two

*Emerging Innovations*

*"To raise new questions, new possibilities,*
*to regard old problems from a new angle, requires creative*
*imagination and marks real advance in science."*
— ALBERT EINSTEIN

Before we get into all the wonderful things you can do for yourself to extend and make your second half of life the best ever, I want to give you some information to make sure you get there. Also, I want you to understand that I am not a doctor or a scientist, but a researcher. All of this information comes from experts in their various scientific and medical fields. Please join me in appreciating all of their work to help us increase our healthy longevity. I write about more about longevity in later chapters, but want to emphasize it here because it is an essential component to keep front and center concerning how you plan your revivement.

## Emerging Innovations for the Bonus Years

While we've been busy becoming older, masterful scientists have been behind the scenes in their labs researching ways to make older better. Let's review a few of the exciting, proven scientific applications that will extend your life and health. These discoveries and new practices are paving the way to our longevity.

*"The brain is wider than the sky."*
— EMILY DICKINSON

We'll start at the top with your brain. Did you know that with advanced biomedical research and health care practices, our bodies can live at least 100 years? Yet, our brains start declining at the age of 40. How can we keep our brains in shape to do our best work, create our highest accomplishments, and savor the latter part of our lives?

Start by adding this word to your vocabulary—neuroplasticity (neuro for "neuron" and plastic for "changeable, malleable, modifiable"). It represents the new brain science that proves that our brains cannot only be smarter and younger, but can help us live longer and healthier. We can actually change our brain's structure and function through our thoughts and activities.

Experts have revised their opinions about our brain. For years, scientists said it was hardwired in early childhood and could not change. New research shows us we can help our brains grow and increase capacity at any age. In fact, extensive research demonstrates that we have an inherent ability to improve our mental and physical life. But, it's up to us to use the tools that make this possible.

Today there is scientifically proven guidance on how to rejuvenate, remodel, and reshape your brain and improve it at any age by doing some of the things I'll describe in this chapter.

A well-known and respected contributor to your brain's future is Dr. Michael Merzenich, a neuroscientist and professor emeritus at the University of California, San Francisco, as well as a world authority on brain plasticity. He authored the book

*Soft Wired: How the New Science of the Brain Plasticity Can Change Your Life.* His book explains how your brain rewires itself across your life span, and describes how to take control of that process.

Dr. Merzenich advises that the brain has powerful resources to help us. If you take care of your brain, it will sustain you. It can "carry you to higher levels of ability in a life marked by justifiably greater self-confidence and more positive good spirits," he writes. Even if you have been dealt a challenging neurological issue, newly-developed, groundbreaking processes can help your brain improve and recover ability. Of course, you need professional and medical guidance to use the right resources for your specific issue.

At same time, Dr. Merzenich advocates that you need to incorporate ongoing brain training into your life so that you retain your vitality and use this powerful resource to make the most of your years.

One of the methods of support is an extensive array of tools on Dr. Merzenich's BrainHQ.com website. This brain-training system has been developed with an international team of top neuroscientists and other brain experts. Research shows cognitive benefits such as better memory and faster processing as well as real-life benefits such as safer driving and better hearing in noisy places.

Other ways to increase brain activity and connect those neurons include pushing your boundaries by incorporating new activities into your days. Do something that stretches you to learn and grow in an area that is either completely different from anything you've done before, or one that extends your learning into what you already enjoy. Read something that's different from what you normally read. Work on remembering the names of people you just met by using mnemonics. Play memory games. There are many tools.

If you would like to read more about the brain's plasticity, another book, *The Brain that Changes Itself: Stories of Personal Triumph from the Frontiers of Brain Science*, by Norman Doidge, will also enlighten you with the amazing possibilities of extending your brain's capability to a ripe old age. Moreover, the book describes fascinating science research that led to recovery for people with brain injuries, abnormal brain development, and other issues. Today, because of applied scientific research, people are living a normal life.

Exciting discoveries by neuroscientists and researchers at major research centers also offer suggestions for keeping our brains in shape. Sandra Bond Chapman, M.D. Chief Director of the Brain Health Center at the University of Texas, says our brains can actually stay vibrant and active into our older years, barring major brain injury or disease. Most importantly, we can make our brains smarter at any age.

According to scientists, every decade after age 20 we lose 2-3% of the blood flow in the brain that supports our thinking processes. On the other hand, re-engaging the brain with complex thinking and other systematic processes can help regain blood flow in a matter of hours—thereby boosting the brain's ability to function at a higher level.

Isn't it exciting to know that improving your life is in your control? And, there is more...

## Keep Your Memory Sharp

Memory loss is one of the top fears people have as they age. Although it is one of the normal signs of aging, memory loss does not mean we've lost the battle to dementia.

Scientists agree that knowledge can be maintained and potentially increased with age. And not recalling information immediately doesn't mean that our memories have disappeared. Information access simply may take longer. At the same time, the brain is wired to be inspired, whereas status quo (and being on "automatic pilot") can slow it down.

There are several ways to keep brains active and sharp. One of the key components of a memory-saving program is to keep the rest of your body healthy. Many medical conditions—from heart disease to depression—can affect your memory.

"Staying physically and mentally active turns out to be among the best prescriptions for maintaining a healthy brain and a resilient memory," according to *Improving Memory: Understanding Age-Related Memory Loss,* Harvard Health Publications, 2012.

Other predictors of brain health include limiting alcohol to one drink a day, refraining from smoking, and maintaining a healthy weight. Eating a balanced diet low in saturated and trans fats is also key. By adopting these healthy behaviors, the fear of memory loss can be a thing of the past.

### Help on the "MEND"

New experiments are leading scientists to find methods for some people to regain lost memory. Dale Bredesen, M.D., is founding president and former CEO of the Buck Institute for Research on Aging in Marin County, California. He is internationally recognized as an expert in the mechanisms of neurodegenerative diseases such as Alzheimer's disease.

Dr. Bredesen published a study demonstrating the ability to reverse diminished memory in people with mild cognitive impairment. Although the study sample was small, the results were startling. Nine of the 10 patients in the study suggest that memory loss may be reversed and improvement sustained with this therapeutic program that involves personalized diet, exercise and supplementation recommendations.

Dr. Bredesen spent over 30 years researching the treatment and prevention of Alzheimer's disease. He recently published study results in the first paper on the reversal of cognitive decline in patients with early Alzheimer's disease and its precursors.

Although Dr. Bredesen cautioned that there is still much to be learned and more extensive clinical trials are needed before this program is ready to be offered to the general public, the results are promising.

One 67-year-old woman in the study had two years of progressive memory loss, which posed a significant challenge at her demanding job. By following his protocol on metabolic enhancement for neuro-degeneration, or MEND, she was able to reverse this impairment. She said her memory is now better than it has been in years.

Dr. Bredesen's new company, MPI Cognition, is training practitioners around the country in his protocol. Further information can be obtained on the company's website at https://www.mpicognition.com.

## The Truth about Aging Brains at Work

Often, lack of information causes concern about how older workers will function in the workplace, let alone in their private lives. Many people just assume the brains of aging people slow down and become less productive, innovative, or effective.

Nothing could be further from the truth. In fact, brains can function better and be more prolific over time. As we age, "the brain begins to compensate by using more of itself," said Bruce Yankner, M.D., Ph.D., professor of genetics and co-director of the Paul F. Glenn Laboratories for the Biological Mechanisms of Aging at Harvard Medical School. He notes that magnetic resonance imaging (MRI) scans taken of a teenager working through a problem show a lot of activity on one side of the prefrontal cortex, the region we use for conscious reasoning. In middle age, the other side of the brain begins to pitch in. In older workers, both sides of the brain share the task equally.

That's why studies have shown that older people have better judgment, are better at making rational decisions, and are more able to screen out negativity than their juniors. Also, inductive and spatial reasoning improve at middle age. Not having these capacities is no fault of those younger. It's just how we all develop. They too will have these magnificent older brains as they age.

Interestingly, the mastery that comes with maturity is also due to changes in our glands as well as in our brains. Declining levels of testosterone — even in women — result in better impulse control. The end of the hormonal roller coaster of pre- and post-menopause may also contribute to emotional stability. After midlife, people are less likely to have emotional

issues like mood swings and neuroses that interfere with
cognitive function.

In addition, mature employees have acquired the ability to
think strategically as well as use their creativity to find and
implement solutions to issues they face. They know how to
interact with others, work as part of a team, and diffuse
conflicts when necessary. They are also great mentors. Why
wouldn't you want someone like that on your team? Someone
like Eva.

## Eva

*Eva walked into her new job as office manager on Monday morning. She was thrilled when she got the job. Her resume highlighted her strengths, including organizational, strategic, and people skills. It also showed her dependability, loyalty, and focus. She is a natural on paper and even more so in person. Eva is 72.*

*"Why isn't she retired?" you might ask. She's finally at the age where she can collect full Social Security and stay home.*

*But Eva doesn't want to stay home. She wants to be where the action is. She wants to be out in the world and interact with people of all ages, races, nationalities, and skill sets. She knows there is more excitement to being involved in the world than just walking her dog every day. Also, she wants to use her skills, energy, and creativity to make a contribution to the world. And she can do that best at her new job. Today, Eva has become one of the most valued members of the company.*

## Six Steps to Keep Your Brain Alive, Alert and Zippy

Whether you work full-time, part-time, or are just reviving, it is vital to incorporate the following skills to keep your brain alive and well for as long as you live. Keeping your brain healthy during revivement can be the difference between "using it or losing it."

**1. Do one thing at a time and avoid distractions.**
Our multi-tasking world (with frequent interruptions) makes this difficult. However, by learning to stay focused without interruption, you will accomplish more. For example, multi-tasking actually destroys the brain's connections and can:

- Cause brain fatigue
- Reduce efficiency
- Lead to confusion
- Increase stress
- Lessen productivity

**2. Focus on priorities.**
"When you're hunting elephants, don't chase rabbits," says Dr. Chapman, Chief Director of the Brain Health Center. The brain's prime time is the first two hours of the day for morning people. Others may find that the last two hours of the day are more productive for people whose circadian rhythm is optimum at night. Find your best time of day and make it work for you.

**3. Develop a system.**
You may ask how you can be successful when so many "nonproductive activities" command your attention? Let's face it, technology constantly solicits us to read,

do, buy, attend. Some offers are helpful, while others are outside our interest but still require us to pay attention. Developing a system can minimize the impact of distracting phone and email solicitations (including opting out from lists that aren't currently relevant to your life).

### 4. Give your brain a break.
The brain absorbs every input and does not differentiate between important and unimportant information. Our brains need downtime—time to have "aha moments." A rested brain will help us be more productive and think deeply, creatively. If we are always interrupted, we cannot generate new ideas to improve our bottom line, whether it's on the job or enjoying a fulfilling revivement.

### 5. Turn off your "automatic pilot."
Take in complex and abstract ideas and synthesize them. We need to be ingenious, creative, insightful, and resourceful. Near-perfect memory doesn't challenge the brain, and rote memorization dulls it, and does not equate to understanding.

### 6. When you take care of your body, you take care of your brain.
Although we often hear the call for basic nutrition and physical exercise, we don't always adhere to what will improve and sustain our health for years to come. Its important to focus on our whole person—brain and body. Add a new incentive for taking care of yourself— your brain's recharged health—which also responds to healthy living. By making brain and health a priority, you'll be maximizing your ability to enjoy a healthy life.

## Our Negative Thoughts Impact Our Lives

Now that we've discussed the physical brain, let's talk about how we provide ourselves with messages that empower or disempower us. Our minds are very powerful. In fact, they are brilliant. They will take what we say and follow our orders. But, like a computer, we need to program them properly.

The truth is, we often give ourselves negative messages. If you use denigrating internal language, such as, "Oh, that was stupid," or, "Why did I do such a dumb thing?" you do yourself a big disservice.

Why do we do this? Often it is because of the messages we got in childhood—sometimes well-meaning or sometimes just mean. As children, we accepted those evaluations, and have been habitually reinforcing those thoughts ever since. This negative thought pattern can continue into our older years, but we can eliminate it and retrain our brains at any age. It's time to think positively!

Being positive and having a good attitude is not about sticking our heads in the sand and ignoring what's going on around us. Instead, it is how we interact with it all.

## You Are What You Think

If you think you are, you are. If you say you can, you can. If you say you can't, you can't. Thinking we are limited is a limiting factor.

Your body, mood, and emotions react to the thoughts that run through your mind. Your reactions to these statements become true because you have instructed your brain to believe they are so.

Physiologically, your brain releases neurotransmitters—chemical messengers—that allow it to communicate with itself and with your nervous system. Neurotransmitters control virtually all of your body's functions, from hormones to digestion to feeling happy, sad, or stressed.

An article titled, "How Your Thoughts Program Your Cells" written by Lynne McTaggart and quoted in the Huffington Post, explains it this way:

> *"There are thousands upon thousands of receptors on each cell in our body. Each receptor is specific to one peptide, or protein. When we have feelings of anger, sadness, guilt, excitement, happiness or nervousness, each separate emotion releases its own flurry of neuropeptides that change the structure of each cell as a whole. Where this gets interesting is when the cells actually divide. If a cell has been exposed to a certain peptide more than others, the new cell that is produced through its division will have more of the receptor that matches with that specific peptide."*

Just as negative feelings can impact you on a cellular level, positive feelings can actually change your physiological make-up. If you want to feel and be positive and use your brain to capacity, it's your job to bring happy and grateful thoughts into your brain. Since every cell is replaced approximately every two months, you have a good chance over time to completely revamp your negative thoughts into positive thoughts and enjoy a happier life.

## Now That You're Reviving, Do You Deserve to Be Happy?

*"When it rains, most birds head for shelter; the eagle is the only bird that, in order to avoid the rain, starts flying above the clouds."*
— Unknown

Do you deserve to be happy? Yes, you do. Is happiness for everyone? Yes, it is, if you choose it. Like everything, it comes from how we live and how we give. It's a state of mind—an open mind—that takes us to joy.

When you are in revivement, you have more time to pay attention to your personal growth; more time to grow your happiness. Whatever you've ignored because you were "too busy" is up for re-evaluation and action to make you into your best self yet. Use this time to get in touch with your essence.

Is life one big happy experience? No, unfortunately, it isn't. We need to earn our happiness.

Here are three major prerequisites:

**1. Attitude** – how you think, act, and talk exemplifies your attitude. The old "glass half-full/half-empty" cliché rings loud and clear when we interact with ourselves and others. This is not Pollyanna talking. Your mind is brilliant. It does what you want it to do. If you want happiness, it is very willing to help you have it. You just need to put the right components in your mind to make it real. You also need to erase the negative messages your mind has replayed over and over during your lifetime, and replace them with positive messages. As you experienced your challenges, have you seen them as teachers or as punishers? Do you learn from them, or do you say "it's not my fault?" You can change how you interact with the world by choosing to change any negative words into positive words. It takes a little practice, but is well worth the result.

**2. Mind thoughts** – again your mind is your guide and servant. If you tell it you're good, you're good. If you tell it you're bad, guess what? It believes everything, because you are its master. Eliminating negative thinking and replacing it with positive thinking will take you to happiness. Here's how: Listen to yourself closely. Whenever you hear a negative statement, mentally erase and replace it with a positive message. The more you replace the negative statements, the better you'll feel about you. Reprogramming one's mind to be positive is vital to a long, happy life.

**3. Learn optimism.** When anything happens, look for the good. Even when the action is hurtful. Look for the lessons, the wisdom, and the experience that this circumstance has brought to you. This doesn't mean you like what happened. It does mean that you see it for what it is and learn from it.

*Joe Henry was an amazing optimist, his daughter told me. Disasters never cost him a night's sleep. He never allowed himself to feel defeated. Joe was the product of Steeltown, Pennsylvania, where his family worked in the factories. They didn't earn enough to feed the family well, but made do. In his lifetime, as a family man, Joe by necessity got very creative about earning money. He tried several jobs, from working at a gas station to plucking turkeys to being a bank teller, a bank manager, and an entrepreneur in several businesses.*

*He even studied law for a while. His multiple careers and pursuits had their ups and downs. In his 70's, in what might to others be retirement age, Joe became enamored with electronic guitars and helped launch a business to restore them. He eventually earned enough money to pay off his mortgage and save for his "old age." Ever optimistic, ever grateful, Joe lived just shy of 94.*

## Do Your Genes Make You Who You Are?

If you think that you've inherited your genetic makeup, and your familial ancestry determines who you are and what you do, then let me introduce you to another new science— Epigenetics, the study of the way in which the expression of heritable traits is modified by environmental influences or other mechanisms without a change to the DNA sequence. In short, we can influence our genes.

Actually, the genes you are born with are responsible for only 25% of how you respond to the world. Scientists, during the past 20 years, discovered that humans are responsible for the rest. They learned the astounding fact that we, as individuals, influence our genes. This is good news. It opens the door to a future of possibilities we didn't even consider.

Just as you can change your brain, you can change your genes. Surprisingly, your genetic makeup plays a small role in your longevity. How long you live has more to do with how you live. So, if you want to live a long, healthy life, you need to change your thinking and behaviors, create a lifestyle that supports long life, and not become a victim to heredity.

The new science of epigenetics also reveals that you are in fact an extension of your environment, which includes everything from your thoughts and belief systems to toxic exposures and exposure to sunlight, exercise, and, of course, everything you choose to put onto and into your body. For example, if you smoke or overeat, you can change the epigenetic marks on your DNA in ways that cause the genes for obesity to express themselves strongly while shortening your life.

In his book *The Genius in All of Us: Why Everything You've Been Told About Genetics, Talent and IQ Is Wrong,* science writer David Shenk says epigenetics is helping usher in a new paradigm that "reveals how bankrupt the phrase 'nature versus nurture' really is." He calls epigenetics, "perhaps the most important discovery in the science of heredity since the gene."

Given these factors, it's clear that you are now in the driver's seat—no longer a passenger without control on your life journey. You can change your brain and your genes, and thereby actually shape your life.

## Longevity—Living Well While Living Long

If you want to know how to live to 100 years plus, ask a centenarian. Studies find commonality in their straightforward responses. They would tell you to live your life well, never smoke, minimize alcohol, and get a good night's sleep. They might suggest you have a positive attitude and be optimistic about life. They also believe you should enjoy your work, work hard, be a lifelong learner, and be involved with your family, friends, and community. In this book, you have already read some of these ideas and will continue to read more about what keeps you healthy on all fronts.

Our centenarians have also been able to enjoy their good, long life because of the many lifesaving and life-extending advancements that have been discovered in the past decades. Advancements in medical care in the last century helped centenarians survive because of progress in infectious disease prevention and treatment.

Among the many medical innovations, this age group has benefited from improved treatment and prevention of childhood diseases, improved practices of maternal health and birthing, polio and other vaccines, antibiotics, heart surgery, cholesterol-lowering medications, and standards of care improvements that include hand washing and sterilization of medical equipment.

Among the more amazing newer advances are new support systems for injured bodies, including robotic limbs for amputees, that are controlled by implants in the brain. This improvement will let a person guide his new limbs more fluidly just by having the intention to move. Another advance includes wearable sensors, which are being developed to help monitor chronic disease conditions. Information derived from these sensors will help improve the control of these illnesses such as diabetes and cardiovascular disease. Soon sensors will be designed into special clothing as well as stick-on tapes and fitness bands.

## How Our Bodies Can Heal and Regrow

Do you like sci-fi movies? Does your imagination grasp the inventive ideas that take you beyond anything you know today? If so, get ready to see these ideas become reality.

Stem cell research has been making the news a lot in the past few years, and there are big hopes for therapies to improve our health and thereby extend our lives. In the future we may be able to use stem cells to help the body heal itself and even grow new limbs and organs, as well as repair damaged tissue.

For instance, in the future, stem cell therapy could prompt the heart to re-grow tissue damaged by a heart attack, and pancreatic beta cells could help people with type 1 diabetes produce their own insulin. Stem cell therapies may also help battle neurodegenerative diseases like Alzheimer's and repair damage caused by a stroke.

You can see why stem cell research gives us hope for therapies that will improve our health and extend our lives. However, repairing and replacing aren't the only goals of regenerative medicine. Stem cells also help researchers study the origin of diseases—how they develop and why—to develop better treatments and focus on prevention. Stem cells can also speed up the development of new drugs because they allow researchers to test new therapies on human tissue—and quickly spot which ones are unsafe so time and money aren't wasted.

## Who's In Charge? Our Genes or Our Food?

Cutting-edge health experts have discovered how the foods we eat interact with our genes to affect our health. This new field of study, called nutrigenomics or nutritional genomics, investigates the amount of each nutrient a particular person should consume, as well as the biological effects of a specific supplement. It tells us why some individuals respond differently than others to the same nutrients.

For instance, some people can eat a high fat diet and have no problem with their cholesterol levels, while others experience the exact opposite response. About 80% of people have a gene that helps the body detoxify some of the harmful chemicals we are exposed to, using a compound found in broccoli and similar vegetables. Although some people won't benefit from the detoxifying properties of broccoli, they are still likely to benefit from its antioxidant effects.

Ahmed El-Sohemy, PhD., one of the world's top nutrigenomics researchers and a pioneer in the field, stated, "we published a study in the Journal of the American Medical Association to demonstrate that in some individuals, caffeinated coffee intake lowered the risk of heart attacks. But in other individuals the same dose of caffeinated coffee increased the risk of heart attacks.

"My lab routinely runs these genetic tests using cells that are easily obtained by swabbing the inside of your mouth. Although this is done primarily for research purposes, we've also developed a test to be used by healthcare practitioners, through a company called Nutrigenomix, that provides individuals with personalized dietary advice based on their genes," he added.

A final example is green tea, which is widely known to have several beneficial phytonutrients, i.e., antioxidants. Interestingly, a number of studies are now showing that some people break down these compounds more slowly and probably don't need to consume as much green tea to get the same benefits.

## Genes and Nutrients

Genes can also affect the foods we select by affecting the brain's reward system. In fact, different nutrients have different effects on neurotransmitters like dopamine and serotonin, both of which influence our mood and behavior. And all of this is based on our genotype. For example, Dr. El-Sohemy's lab investigated why some individuals seem to crave sugars or carbohydrates more than others and why caffeine improves mood in some people but causes anxiety in others.

"I think there's still so much that we don't understand in terms of how nutrients interact with genes to affect health, fitness, and performance. In fact, we're only beginning to appreciate the complexity of the human genome," stated Dr. El-Sohemy.

"We used to think that any two individuals were 99.9% the same, but it looks like we're probably much more different from one another. As our understanding of the human genome improves, it changes the types of questions we start asking about nutrition, and it changes how we design our studies."

In fact, for example, there are about two-dozen genes that code for bitter taste receptors on the surface of the tongue. Variations in these genes could explain why some people find certain foods like broccoli or cauliflower very bitter, yet others find them delicious.

Dr. El-Sohemy concluded, "As for other areas of nutrition research, I think we're going to start seeing some very interesting work involving the application of nanoscience. This will involve changes to the delivery system of nutrients and food bioactives."

For individuals looking for a more personalized approach to healthy eating for overall wellness, you can find an authorized provider of Nutrigenomix (www.nutrigenomix.com).

These are but a few of the exciting innovations being discovered to make longevity a reality. These advances have conspired to give us the grand opportunity of having a long, good life. Why would we ever want to retire completely? Instead, we need to learn to just flow from one life scene to another with confidence that we will be adapting to a healthy and meaningful lifespan.

My website features information about the latest research and discoveries that help us age healthily. Subscribe to Revivement Reviews at www.havingalifenow.com.

# Chapter
# Three

*Honoring Work*

*"Your work is going to fill a large part of your life, and the only way to be truly satisfied is to do what you believe is great work. And the only way to do great work is to love what you do."*

— STEVE JOBS, CO-FOUNDER & CEO OF APPLE

We, who are over 50, have increasingly realized the worth of our minds, our wills, and our skills. And we know we will keep growing in these areas our entire life. We also know that although our bodies may flag, the essential part of us is strong and resilient. And, we still have a lot to contribute to mankind.

We older adults are also catching on to the fact that working into our later years is a gift we give to others and ourselves. We don't need to stop. We just need to modify how much time and energy we want to "work."

We also need to reframe the word work so that it has a positive and uplifting connotation. For too long it has been cast as the daily grind. And, for many it was. But, I say we change that view now that you're in charge of your work life, and you look at it as the opportunity to express yourself if you choose to continue working.

## Shirley

*Shirley, at 90, doesn't want to change anything about her work life. She buzzes up and down the California freeway selling houses and property. Her knowledge, experience, and customer service have made her a star performer in real estate for the past 50 years.*

*When Shirley semi-retired ("Retire? Never!!!") she moved to a second home she had purchased as an investment 20 years before in the Sierra Nevada foothills. She kept her first home in Marin County, 250 miles away, where her client base resided. When she moved to her second home, she continued to commute between her homes. She added new clients in her new location, but didn't want to desert the ones who had counted on her over the years. Some clients had bought and sold their houses three times with her professional advice and support.*

*While Shirley does not work full-time anymore, she says, "It energizes me to be involved in helping someone find the right home. I look forward to each day, thinking about what I can do to further someone's life in a positive way. My contribution is my background in real estate. I understand the market. I know the territory. And I know how to put a deal together." Shirley doesn't limit her contributions to her business. She belongs to service organizations and is involved in her community. Her social life includes travel, theater, and visiting with friends. She's also an ace poker player. Her age has not dampened her enthusiasm. She has a rich life.*

Some older action-takers such as Shirley are able to transition to part-time or project work based on their former careers. Others need to express newly discovered talents and skills.

### Keith

*Keith is 64, and was a practicing orthopedist for four decades. He told me he always wanted to act in the theater, but didn't know if he had talent. He wanted to check out this calling on his bucket list, so he decided to enroll in a community college theater course to find out. Today, at his local community and college theaters, he is playing leading or secondary roles while learning his new craft. "This certainly gets me up in the morning," he says. "After all, if I'm not in class or on the stage, I'm practicing my lines, doing voice exercises, or imagining scenes in my mind." Keith also volunteers at a local medical clinic 10 hours a week. "I feel like my life is pretty full right now."*

Now, while I don't want to disparage individuals who did all the "right" things and are now enjoying the revivement for which they worked, I want to emphasize that retiring from paid work does not mean you're done. That's why I use the term "revivement." People like Shirley and Keith are among the thousands of older adults who have learned how to have a life. They've incorporated what they knew with what they wanted to know, and have created new lives. They may have struggled during their first days of adjustment. Their moods may have been on a roller coaster. Or, they might have jumped into the change easily. I applaud them. They are now enjoying life. After all, isn't that the goal? For them, just having the old lingo for their new way of being didn't change the desired result. Good for them for figuring out their lives and being front-runners!

But, for the rest of us, let's get the word retirement (which means end, over, done) out of our vocabulary. Who would ever want to retire? Remember, our new word is revivement. Let's honor not only how far we've come, but also our age. Let's call ourselves revivers and revelers in our futures.

I hope to encourage everyone to have the fullest life possible, no matter what age. I hope to inspire those who love their work to keep working, just on their terms. And, I honor those who no longer want to work. After all, it's all about choice. As I said earlier, I want to bust the idea of a certain age being a definitive end point to life based on the old philosophy of retirement and Social Security. My goal is to support you wherever you are to have the best life possible—your way.

Work that is meaningful to you—paid or unpaid—provides you with an opportunity to put purpose into practice. Work you love allows you to use the inherent and learned skills you've honed over a lifetime and ensures a satisfying life.

I believe the workplace is a playground for our talents, and that our work can encourage us to grow personally and professionally. The lessons we learn through work can't be acquired just by sitting at home alone, but rather, we need to pay attention.

Where else besides work do you mix with people who are so different from you in personality, mannerisms, values, and backgrounds? To get the job done, you need to learn to respect and work with them. What other entity besides work tests you and your skills to reach a goal and attain an end result? Who else challenges your dependability, commitment, and focus? What arena gives you the opportunity to fail and learn from your failures, as well as reap huge rewards for your efforts and win?

Although you have exercises in the back of this book to guide you throughout your revivement, here is a preliminary question to help you understand why this book is relevant to you. Ask yourself what lessons you've learned from the many places you have worked. Can you not see the value? Make a list of each job/career and the good you received from being in that space at that time. Yes, there were difficulties too, and you can list them.

What I want to underscore here are the take-aways—the gifts that help you be who you are today. It's because of the workplace that you have evolved into who you are. All you have learned you can now take forward and use for your grand plan.

Now, not everyone enjoys work or wants to continue a work lifestyle. Understood! At the same time, many of us over the age of 50 who don't want to sit on a porch and knit. Sure, we like the freedom of what some call 'retirement' – meaning you don't have to punch a company time clock anymore. And, we want to spend quality time with our families and friends. We want to play, whether it's golf, tennis, or travel. But some of us also actually want to work because for us, work is play. Work can be a way to produce a meaningful end result by doing something we love.  By now, we have learned how to balance our lives by doing what's important to us. And some of us still need to earn money.

"In search of purpose, you might want to work in your 60s, 70s, and beyond—for both means and meaning. You might be interested in an encore career, using your experience to help solve problems in areas like education, health and the environment. An accumulation of research suggests the payoff includes continued mental and physical vitality," writes Marc Freedman, CEO and Founder of Encore.org.

Ninety-eight percent of us have a deep-seated need to experience work as meaningful, reports the Gallup Organization. In addition, Dr. Teresa Amabile, Professor and Director and Research at Harvard Business School and her team of researchers, established that when we view work as meaningful, we experience joy and excitement. If you work with purpose, you will exude enthusiasm, energy, and passion. You will feel involved, committed, and focused. Working with a sense of meaning and purpose affords more than a connection to high ideals. It expands and extends life.

People who derive meaning and significance from their work are more than three times as likely to stay with their organizations. But, across 142 countries, the proportion of employees who feel engaged at work is only 13 percent. And, according to a 2016 Gallup report, only 32.6 percent of employees in America feel engaged at work.

In their book *The Why of Work*, Dave and Wendy Ulrich explain that there are many advantages to helping people find purpose in a job. On an individual level, people who understand how their jobs fit into an organizational purpose are happier, more engaged, and more creative. People work harder, use their initiative, and make sensible decisions about their work. In turn, the company can operate more efficiently. Everyone, from the CEO to customers, feels the positive effects.

Today, about half of the National Institute of Health's (NIH) 20,000 employees are over 50. Older workers range from bench scientists doing biomedical lab work to administrative professionals in human resources—to doctors and nurses in the NIH hospital. The average age of an NIH employee is 48.

Dr. Herbert Tabor, a distinguished 95-year-old biomedical researcher, was honored for 70 years of service. By comparison, 83-year-old Dr. Thomas Waldmann, world renowned in the field of immunology, is a relative newcomer, arriving at the NIH during the Eisenhower Administration. His discoveries led to clinical trials and treatments for various diseases.

"It's like dominoes. You never finish. You always want to see projects to the end," Waldmann says. "When you see a patient who's alive who might not have been without some of your drug therapy, it's a thrill." He has no plans to retire. This is a great example of purposeful living!

Did you ever want to be something or do something you just haven't gotten around to doing yet? Maybe you think you're too old. Well, old is not in the new revivement vocabulary. Nor is age!

In my view, once you are by choice not working at a job full-time, or even part-time, you can absorb life's meaning, be involved in personally fulfilling projects, and create the life you want. Then you can add work back into the equation if it fits.

To me, work must be something you love doing. It is an avocation you get paid for, yet the pay you enjoy the most is the good feeling inside yourself.

If you want to make a dramatic shift, you can have your work be something totally different than anything you've ever done—like the CEO who becomes a sculptor, or the TV anchor who becomes a restaurant owner. Different decision-making avenues take these individuals to places within themselves.

### Marty

*Marty was a successful engineer who retired and became a mailman. He would tell you that he has spent his life inside his head figuring out issues in an office cubicle. Now, in his revivement, he just wants to be outdoors and doing something that gives him exercise and a reason to get up every day. He might decide after a few years that he filled that need, and it's time to go in a new direction. The beauty of revivement is you get to explore whatever your heart desires.*

## Work Options

Should you want to continue working, today you get to select from a list of options. For instance, if you don't want to work full-time any more, yet you like the work you do, consider phased retirement by slowly cutting back your hours to what feels right for you. Consider new pension freedoms that allow you to combine pension income with earnings and therefore plan a gradual retirement. This works great for those who want to ease into their future slowly.

Today some companies offer flexible work arrangements and hours to their staff. These can include part-time employment, compressed work schedules, job-sharing, changing jobs within the same company, telework arrangements, so-called snowbird programs (which allow employees to shuttle between two locations seasonally), and hiring former employees as independent contractors.

## Reinventing your work

Another common option among retiring employees is called "re-careering," otherwise known as career change. According to AARP, "Half of the workers who left their career jobs by the time they were ages 65 to 69 moved to a new employer; nearly two thirds of those were re-careerers. For many, this meant downshifting to less demanding jobs with lower wages and fewer benefits, but more flexibility. Workers overwhelmingly enjoy their new jobs." What does that tell us? Flexibility and employment are a good match.

## How not to retire

What if you most definitely do not want to work? Guess what? If you have the means to support yourself with Social Security, a pension, and savings, you don't have to. It's a choice. But a question then is, "How will you fill your hours every day?" In other words, what will give you a sense of purpose and meaning? What will you do to replace the parts of your job that you enjoyed?

Look into my crystal ball and see your "workless" future. What are you doing as a retiree? Are you happy? Are you satisfied? Or are you questioning your everyday existence?

So, you don't want to get a job. Okay! But, you could say to yourself, "I do have things I'd like to do. Maybe I'll start my own business. I'll become an entrepreneur." Do you know that people over 50 are actually exiting the formal workplace to become entrepreneurs? In fact, businesses started by those ages 55 to 64 account for nearly one-fourth of all new companies.

An article in the *New York Times* titled "Why Innovators Get Better With Age," written by Benjamin Jones of Northwestern University, stated that a 55-year-old and even a 65-year-old have significantly more innovation potential than a 25-year-old.

This was confirmed by one of Germany's largest companies. Their internal survey showed that older workers not only had great ideas for making procedures and processes more efficient, but their innovations also produced significantly higher returns for the company than those of workers in younger age groups.

At the same time, Duke University scholar Vivek Wadhwa, who studied 549 successful technology ventures, tells us that older entrepreneurs have higher success rates when they start companies. Although true of all industries, she focused on technological fields. She said these older workers have accumulated expertise and deep knowledge of their customers' needs. They also have developed a network of supporters (often including financial backers). "Older entrepreneurs are just able to build companies that are more advanced in their technology and more sophisticated in the way they deal with customers," she added.

Overall, the 50-plus generation will be making major contributions to the global economy for decades to come as they use their skills to innovate and develop products and services to meet the needs of their peers. They understand this growing marketplace and how to produce deliverables that sell.

If there is anything you ever wished you could do to have your own business, now is the time, this is the place, and you are it. There are so many stories about people who created their own businesses or own jobs. See a need and fill it. Let your imagination run wild. Then make it happen.

On the other hand, if you are enjoying your life without working, keep doing what you're doing. You have a right to have your life be your way. The bottom line is to make sure you are satisfied, happy, and fulfilled.

## How Companies Can Win Too

If companies understand and act on the needs of reviving employees, they will benefit as well. With the looming shortage of workers, especially in certain fields, companies don't want to lose their experienced and skilled employees no matter their age.

Wise companies are trying to help themselves by employing the over-60 age group by redesigning work flow and expectations to meet the needs of today's older workforce.

Many older employees have honed their skills for 40 years, a reliable and proven resource the business sector can no longer disregard. Nothing beats experience.

Our country as a whole is waking up to this fact, too. With funding from the Sloan Foundation, the Associated Press-NORC Center for Public Affairs Research conducted a national survey of 1,024 adults ages 50 and over. They found that there is a shift, if slow-moving, in the American idea of retirement. They found that retirement is not only beginning later in life, but for many it no longer represents a complete exit from the workforce.

Hiring the mature worker, in my opinion, can bring a financial boost to both workers and the economy. It's a win-win. Workers get to use their skills and make meaningful contributions, which enhance their lives. And employers get to utilize the abundance of skills these workers provide and enjoy greater business success.

The truth is, we need everyone. Older workers do not replace younger workers, but they are great mentors and supporters of aspiring professionals. With guidance, emerging professionals can focus on increasing their abilities and produce outcomes in less time and with less stress.

An additional bonus to an older workforce is that the more income available to our older population through salaries, the more they have available to spend, which can boost the economy and benefit more people.

# Chapter
# Four

*Change—Loss or Gain*

*"When we change the way we look at things,
the things we look at change"*

— WAYNE DYER, AUTHOR AND SPEAKER

Revivement is a major change that we often expect will just
fall into place after our final days at work. Unfortunately, it's
not that easy. Thousands of retirees struggle with what to do
with their lives after they no longer have work goals,
meetings, and all of the other activities that fill their job
descriptions. Why? Because most changes knock us out of our
comfort zones and we resist trying out a new lifestyle, new
behavior, or new thinking.

Let's be honest. Change is uncomfortable. Many of us stay
stuck in the status quo because we fear change. We don't
know what to expect, how things will resolve themselves, or
what will happen to us. So we delay, ignore, or rationalize our
circumstances to avoid change. If you experience a feeling of
loss after you retire, know that it is natural. But status quo
doesn't work for new revivers. It dulls their existence.

Revivers need to adapt to their new lives, and for some it isn't
easy. Especially if a certain career path or behavior style has

been their life for 20, 30, 40 or more years. Whether or not you are already retired or anticipate an emptiness in your life, you may need to grieve. Don't be surprised if you go through some or all of the emotions.

While Elisabeth Kübler-Ross, M.D. originally developed a model  to deal with end of life issues in her book on *Death and Dying,* these stages were never intended to be a rigid framework that applies to everyone who mourns. They simply give us a way of understanding the emotional side of loss.

In her last book before her death in 2004, she said of the five stages of grief: "They were never meant to help tuck messy emotions into neat packages. They are responses to loss that many people have, but there is not a typical response to loss, as there are no typical losses. Our grieving is as individual as our lives." And it's only natural to grieve for a career you no longer have.

## The emotional stages are:

**Denial**—"This can't be happening to me."
The first reaction is denial. In this stage individuals believe that how they feel once retired is a mistake and are confused.

**Anger** —"Why is this happening? Who is to blame?"
Once the retiree recognizes that denial cannot continue, he or she becomes frustrated, especially at others. Certain psychological responses of a person undergoing this phase would be: "Why me? It's not fair!" "How can this happen to me?" "Who is to blame?" "Why would this happen?"

**Bargaining**—"Make this not happen, and in return, I will give you anything you want."
The third stage involves the hope that the individual can avoid

a cause of grief. Usually, the negotiation for an extended life is made in exchange for a reformed lifestyle. People facing less serious trauma might bargain or seek compromise.

**Depression** "I'm too sad to do anything."
"I'm so sad, why bother with anything? I'm going to die soon anyway, so what's the point? I miss what I had. Why go on?" During the fourth stage, the individual despairs at the recognition of their mortality. In this state, the individual may become isolated, begin drinking, watching a lot of television, gambling and other mind-numbing activities.

**Acceptance** – "Everything is going to be okay. I can see the light at the end of the tunnel, and it's shining bright for me."
"I'm at peace with what happened."
Finally: "It's going to be okay." "I can't fight it, so I may as well prepare for it."

If you're reading this book before you retire and don't want to be debilitated by change, then become aware of the stages now so you can ride the waves of change, and get to the other side. If you're reading this book after you've retired, go back over each stage and honor it with what you've been through. Once you've allowed yourself to grieve, you can let go of what was and get onto what will be. You will come out on a higher plane of understanding about yourself, and you will find joy in your new life. The exercises in the back of this book can help you work through feelings about your transition to revivement.

Remember, once you've traveled down the same road for many years, changing direction is hard. You've become accustomed to your pattern and schedule. You recognize people, places, processes, practices, and norms you've experienced for decades. Although you may struggle within these confines, you are comfortable with what you know. It's as if you've been traveling north, and in the blink of an eye, you are forced to travel east. It can feel like moving to a new country or even exploring a new planet. And, it requires rethinking every aspect of your life.

When you retire from a job, an employer, a set of coworkers that you've been with for a period of time, you are making a dramatic change and may not know what to expect. You need to explore a whole new way of being in the world. How you go about it is up to you. The truth is, as Henry David Thoreau ponders, "Things do not change; we change."

One way to approach a big change is by asking yourself: What are the things you lost that you are glad to give up? What are the things you no longer have that you want to replace? Sometimes after we end a marriage, we hope to find a new mate. It took me 20 years after I divorced my first husband to find the second one, and it was worth the process I went through to learn and grow on the way. My second husband and I have now been together 21 years. But, I do understand the difficulties.

Here are a few routes to take on your after-worklife journey:

**1. Awareness.**
If you don't know what's holding you back, you will stay stuck. The first step in any endeavor is being aware. Lack of awareness causes us to trip over ourselves as we reach out for what we want. Retirement/revivement can create a vacuum if you don't have a plan to fill your days. You want to think through what your days and weeks will be like without your job, and fill them with activities that are pleasurable and fulfilling.

## 2. Attitude

This trait will help you accomplish whatever you set your mind to do. Go into revivement understanding that you will be a work in progress as you traverse this new territory. Envision that your cup is half-full instead of half- empty.

## 3. Ownership

If you don't own your process, someone else will lead you where you don't want to go. Because you have acquired a wide breadth of skills during your work years, you may be called on to volunteer, serve on boards, and otherwise give over control of your newly found time. These are worthy undertakings when we have time to give back, but, it's important to be careful how many times you say "yes."

## 4. Intention

It's easy to become scattered unless you pull all your internal resources together and focus on your desired results. Go for what you really want by having a clear intention. Be your own boss with a project, and focus on it. Whether the project is going back to school, taking art classes, or working part-time at a new profession, give it your full intention and make it successful.

## 5. Action

If you don't act, you don't get. Move toward your desired outcome and reap the rewards. You don't have to make a mad dash to reach this destination. Take it slowly if you need to.

### 6. Enjoy the Journey

Remember that wholeness comes from integrating your new "transition adventure" with the other important aspects of your life. Don't wait for an end point. Instead enjoy each step along the way.

Navigate this major transition as you would navigate an important work project by planning and taking action. Incorporate purposeful activities and experiences. Then, get ready to experience a fulfilling and exciting future!

# Chapter
## Five

*Planning the Rest of Your Life*

> *"Life isn't about finding yourself.
> Life is about creating yourself."*
>
> —GEORGE BERNARD SHAW

Revivement is like a puzzle. You have hundreds of puzzle pieces within you that are encoded with skills, desires, and interests. You need to bring them out to play, and decide which ones to match up. When you engage in using them, you feel good because they have become part of you. Now you need to put them together in a plan and honor them with action. Complete the puzzle and you'll get the picture. Does spending the rest of your life lying on the beach appeal to you? How about reviewing files that filled your business cabinets and are now obsolete? No! I didn't think so.

People who revive without an active plan end up with empty days, which add up to empty years and even decades. Their time is now open-ended, and they don't know what to do with it or themselves. Some try idle busyness, finding things to fill the time, or use that awful phrase, "killing time." But those things are not satisfying. It's easy to become depressed when there's nothing in your life that is fulfilling.

Think of it this way. You may no longer have your usual paid work to fill your hours. Some of your contacts will be lost as you move on. You might even miss going to meetings. Okay, not likely, but you never know. Meetings don't only tease your brain, they give you social time with coworkers and colleagues. The work parties, social outings, teamwork, will be gone. Now who are you going to play with?

I urge revivers to make sure they have a good group of friends to support them and to challenge themselves to try new things, learn new skills, and develop resourcefulness in everyday situations. I also urge them to stay in the moment and be present instead of revisiting past issues that will never be resolved. Mostly, I suggest they, and you, find purpose and meaning in life today by focusing on something larger than yourself, while letting your gifts come from within. Developing your personal life plan will help you create a satisfying revivement, in part because this is uncharted territory for you. You've been acculturated to save money, buy insurance, pay taxes, and if possible, own a home. But you probably were not taught to have a life plan. Now that you are going to live another 30 to 40 more years after the traditional retirement age, it is essential to design a plan to help adjust to a new life after retirement.

## Why You Need a Plan

- Reduces anxiety of the unknown
- Provides direction and how-to's
- Paints a picture of what's possible
- Breaks down activities into small achievable bites
- Wakes up your motivation to move forward
- Becomes a friend and guide that you interact with
- Offers flexibility to change where needed
- Helps you experience progress
- Rewards you as you achieve goals
- Allows you to enjoy successful outcomes
- Helps you become the person you are meant to be
- Allows you to have the life you are meant to have

You will do well by planning your future. You will successfully follow your intended path into your future with a sense of comfort and assuredness that you will succeed. If you do the work, it will work for you. The exercises in the back of the book support your plan.

## Men Have a Harder Time

In addition to the cautionary stories you've already read, let me tell you what happened to Charlie, who did not have an action plan to step into after he retired.

### *Charlie*

*A high-level CEO, Charlie had worked for 46 years building his printing business. He expanded the reach of his company across the United States, owning 58 franchises. He was a take-charge and make-it-work guy and accrued substantial money to leave his heirs.*

*After he retired, he still got up early every day, seven days a week, and then went to his home office. There he fiddled with old files, read newspapers, and checked old financial reports. He needed something to do, and that was all he knew.*

*After a while, he decided his family needed to take advantage of his business acumen, and he started querying his adult children on their various careers and businesses. He would grill them and give them his unasked-for advice. It was not appreciated. Not knowing what to do with his retirement, he got into everyone else's business, causing animosity and anger. As he became more demanding about how his family members and others were leading their lives, they started staying away from him, and became estranged.*

*Finally, Charlie decided to become a day trader, buying and selling stocks, a risky proposition for even the most financially savvy among us. Within six months he lost everything. He died three months later of a heart attack—a miserable, confused, annoying man.*

*Had Charlie planned for his retirement and learned how to use his time and money to contribute to his family and the world, this scenario could have ended much differently, and much happier.*

Here's another story:

### George and Ginny

*At age 60, when George lost his bid for promotion, he was devastated. As an associate manager, he expected a move up to the top manager position.*

*When his secretary Ginny opened his office door, she found him sitting at his desk with his head in his hands moaning about being passed over for advancement. "Why?" he said in a distraught voice. "I've been working all these years only to be passed up by a guy from the outside? I don't understand."*

*It was difficult for Ginny to see this usually strong, in-charge, intelligent man reduced to wobbly jello. He was so deflated. She thought she saw tears running down his cheeks. "So sad," she thought.*

*Ginny realized how lucky she was to not be so attached to her job. While work was her boss's 24/7 existence, she had other interests and activities outside of work to balance her life.*

If tears are the reaction to an unpleasant outcome while still in your job, you can imagine what it is like when a man retires after spending 30-to-50 years defining himself by his work. Without a plan, retirement means an unknown future. That's why I have exercises in the back of this book that will help you renegotiate who you are so you see your value and know how to transition your skills and talents to a new life focus.

As a caveat, some women also tie their total sense of self to a job or career. But we find that it happens to men more often because they have been socialized to find personal value through their accomplishments at work.

For instance, Charlie, like many men who grew up early in the 20th century, was socialized to play a certain role. He was supposed to work, come home with a paycheck, discipline the children, and go back to work the next day. Women were the

homemakers. In fact, when I grew up, what I knew was that I was supposed to get married, have a family, and live happily ever after. After all, TV families used to show us that lifestyle script. So I bought it.

Over the years, I learned through books and magazines that there were other possibilities for my life. I didn't have to follow the "script," but it wasn't until something inside me pushed me to be and do more that I even realized I wanted to finish college, which led to my first career. I was fortunate to have the women's movement teach me that I was more than my socialized role. Men didn't get that kind of support.

We see older, retired men everywhere who look lost. The what-do-I-do-now syndrome seems at this point to affect men more. They not only bought the script when they began their jobs, but continued to reinforce it their entire careers. After all, that is all they knew. And today, many men still don't know how to transition into their newly retired lives. Sometimes, if they are married, they invade their wife's territory at home or join the club or organization where she had carved out her own separate identity.

In fact, some men who don't know how to make this big transition to figuring out their own lives, decide it is time for them to manage their spouse. That usually causes strife, or worse, divorce.

As a man, you need to advance your revivement transition with gusto as if it is a new job. Because it is! It's the job of becoming the man who makes his life happen now by going through the strategic steps to reach his goals. It's the man who puts action into his plans and expects results. It's the man who feels accomplished because he has engineered his life to be fulfilling.

Remember how you used to tackle a challenging work project? Use these same skills to take on your plan for revivement. If you have lost your social contacts from work, find organizations with activities that interest you. Find buddies that you can socialize and play poker with, go for a hike, go sailing. There are thousands of activities available to you. You are now in charge to design your days for pleasure. Figure out how, just like you would figure out a work project.

Then, join one or two volunteer organizations to fill your need for purpose and meaning, and get involved. You have so many skills you've acquired in the workplace, and volunteering is a great place to use them. At the same time, you will add to your social network by engaging with other like-minded volunteers.

Another secret to having an active life is to eliminate sleeping late and watching too much TV. Instead, plan your sleeping time so you can get up early enough to get ready for your day. As one man told me, "I get up every morning as if I'm going to my job. I shave, get dressed, and get out of the house." Now, you don't have to shave every day, but getting out of the house is a good idea. Yes, you can still sit at the kitchen table with a cup of coffee and a newspaper first thing. Then be on your way to make your life happen. Of course, it's important to not get too structured. You can have just hanging out and doing nothing days, too. It's up to you to figure out what the best mix of activity and downtime is. I just want you to see it isn't that difficult to make revivement work.

Again, exercises at the back of this book will help you identify the best activities, volunteer projects and other decisions for you. Read this book first so you get the full picture, then do the worksheets and find your path to revivement.

## How Couples Make it Work

*"The meeting of two personalities is like the contact of two chemical substances: if there is any reaction, both are transformed."*

— C. J. Jung

At a meeting I attended, one of the male members got up to announce he was retiring. "But," he said, "my wife said, don't come home." Of course, everyone laughed. But I'm sure she wasn't kidding.

### Anne

*Living together after retirement is a challenge. "It's disruptive," said 70-year-old Anne. "My husband and I have an expression that it's like when someone stands up in a canoe and throws all the balance off. You need to figure out how to re-stabilize the boat or you'll sink."*

*Anne's husband, Vic, retired some time before she did. He had the house routine down and felt he owned the home territory. He did the grocery shopping, laundry, gardening, maintenance, and took out the garbage. She cooked and entertained. But that was about it.*

*Initially, she had a computer set up in their study. He wasn't computer-savvy early on, so she had it all to herself. But he caught up, and all of a sudden he made the computer room his own. The couple began to bicker over computer access, and when Anne retired, the bickering ballooned into heated arguments. The couple worked through their disagreements, and as Anne described, "It's been interesting getting used to dancing around our space. It's been three years, and we're getting pretty good," she said.*

### Nat and Nancy

*Another couple had a major disruption in their lives when Nat, who had been a top manager at a major corporation, ended his work years. With ten employees reporting directly to him, he was used to the role of leader: making decisions, directing people's work, setting goals, and measuring outcomes. He had organizational goals, strategies, and tactics to achieve. He had deadlines to meet. Those were the skills he banked on to stimulate activity and produce his company's services and products. Suddenly, the environment and people he worked with were gone. His image as a competent and successful leader was gone. Now what?*

*"It was like he was running 90 miles an hour and then fell off a cliff," said his wife Nancy, when describing her husband's first months of retirement.*

*"Everything is programmed for you at work," said Nat. "I had a staff to support my department's mission. Now, I didn't know what to do." He hated the word retirement. He hated the idea of being retired. In fact, he didn't admit it to anyone for years. He used to have an awesome job. Now he didn't feel productive and useful.*

*"I felt I lost 80% of my persona. Who was I now? My career defined who I was. After retirement, I felt like a nobody."*

*"It was like he had to hit bottom after falling off the cliff before he could begin to rebuild his life into what we have today," said Nancy.*

*The first three years of the couple's retirement were not easy. Nat was restless. He brought his management skills home and started supervising Nancy. She started balking. Not a good scene. Nancy did fine when she was on her own, and did not need a boss now. After an argument, both would go to their corners, exhausted and miserable.*

*When Nat realized he was jeopardizing his marriage, he decided to go work for a friend. That didn't work either. Quarrels erupted like volcanoes. He needed to find another outlet.*

*He was, unfortunately, not alone in his conundrum. Unless a couple adapts to their jobless lifestyle, they are headed for divorce.*

*Nat and Nancy were wise, and they decided to talk about their new life and how they wanted to make it work. They realized they wanted to be together, but they were both going to need to change.*

*Communication was key in the next few years as they expressed their needs, their likes, and their dislikes. They planned what they wanted their lives to be like. After a lot of discussion, they agreed they wanted to stay together. But, they knew that honest communication would be key in saving their marriage. It would no longer work to politely dance around their personal frustrations or hold back on their real needs. They set up a schedule to focus their conversation on their future together. They committed three days a week for two-hour intervals (except when traveling) to sit at the kitchen table with a big pad and honest conversation.*

*One of the steps they took was to sell their big house and let go of all the gardening. They downsized to a home that would take less caretaking time so they could travel.*

*They also found they could have their independent time and together time. Actually, it made life more interesting to have his, hers, and their activities. Nat joined a men's club that offers 30 small group options for activities from fly fishing to golf to poker. Nancy continued her volunteer and women's group activities. At the same time, they enjoy travel, visiting grandkids, and going out to dinner. Coming home with new ideas to share enriches their conversations.*

*They compromised and made agreements that have become the cornerstone of their happy marriage.*

Some suggestions from Nat and Nancy:

1. Don't wait until you retire to figure out how to revive together. Start planning early.
2. Transition from a full-time job to part-time. Find short-term jobs and projects.
3. Don't underestimate how hard it is to transition from the role you've played—managing others, overseeing a product launch—to now just you making the decisions for your life.
4. Acknowledge you are in for a big change. Don't underestimate the impact it will have on you and your lives together. "This is huge," said Nat. "It's as big a change for the spouse as it is for the retired partner."
5. Discuss your relationship. There is nothing wrong with admitting your mistakes.
6. Communicate about what is working and what isn't without making each other wrong. Honor that each person has a right to his or her own perspective.
7. Find things you and your spouse can do and enjoy together as well as individual pursuits you can do independently. A mixture of his, hers and theirs provides for a healthy relationship.
8. Downsize your residence and be free from a lot of maintenance and gardening so you can travel when you want to.
9. Develop a new living space together and configure personal space and shared responsibilities.
10. Maintain your connections to the people you are close to from work, especially if you spent many years socializing with them.
11. Become best friends with each other.
12. Put new life pursuits in place to replace what was there before.
13. Share together the magnitude of the change.
14. Communicate about every aspect.

Additionally, know yourself and your own expectations as well as your willingness to compromise and go for a win-win resolution that works for both of you. If you need a third party to help guide you and help you plan this new way of life, use a coach or therapist. Just saying "we'll travel and see the grandkids" isn't enough. Also use this third party to help you acquire communication skills, which include listening, and conflict resolution skills, which includes blame-free discussion. Also, acknowledge each person's contribution to the sanctity of your marriage or partnership.

Remember, no matter how much you love each other, most people need some personal space—alone time at home, alone time to think, alone time to be. Being together 24/7 can get annoying.

Nancy and Nat can tell you it wasn't easy, but they took big steps and corrected their revivement dysfunction. It took them three years to work everything out by themselves. Nancy described this change in their lives as two trains heading toward each other that learned to run on parallel tracks.

In sum, plan. Don't wait until you or your spouse retires before putting a new life plan in place. Know there might be some rough patches to defining your future, but be willing to work them out. You will find that planning and communicating the truth about what you want your next 30-40 years to be like will enhance your relationship and bring peace to the rest of your life.

## What if you're single?

*I celebrate myself, and sing myself.*
—WALT WHITMAN

You might think it is easier for single people—whether divorced, widowed or unmarried—to retire without the challenges of a spouse. Not for Elsa, it wasn't.

### Elsa

*Elsa was a CPA for a large financial firm. At 62, her children were grown and on their own. She had done her best raising them while working full-time. But, she was tired of the daily grind—on the road at 6 am, home at 6 pm. She was tired of the politics and disputes in her office. Mostly, she was tired of working for a boss who didn't value her. During her 20 years in the firm, the stress took its toll. She had stomach pains, pneumonia, and other ailments. So her time off was usually spent flat on her back in bed.*

*The idea of retirement was constantly on her mind. "Oh, some day I'll retire and get out of here," she thought. Given her age, that day loomed large in her view. "Just hang on," she would say to herself. "I'll be out of here soon."*

*Through the years she had juggled work and family as a single mom. Now that the kids were off to their own adult lives, she kept thinking she was going to enjoy her space and her time without interference. Like most people, the idea of retirement was like a carrot on a stick held just beyond reach until that magic day when all would be well again.*

*The day came. Elsa retired. Now what? Elsa had not taken the time to plan her retirement. All of a sudden her days were long and boring. Mostly, she didn't know what to do with this gift of time.*

*One day, Elsa remembered her friend Gladys, the director of a volunteer organization that helps underserved families with food, medical care, and social support. Over the years, Gladys had invited Elsa to volunteer, but Elsa was always too busy, too stressed or sick.*

*After a conversation with Gladys, Elsa learned that she could attend a meeting for new volunteers the coming Thursday at 10 am. She whipped out her calendar and jotted down the pertinent information. Whew, something on her calendar to look forward to.*

*Gladys also suggested they meet for coffee so she could tell Elsa about some of the other activities that keep her busy and satisfied. They set a date for Tuesday at 9 am. Wow, now two things on her calendar.*

*Here was a clue! Elsa realized that some of her retired friends might also be able to tell her about how they spend their days. She called Sally, Fran, and Harry. Yes, even Harry seemed happily busy in his revivement. All of a sudden she had coffee and lunch dates that would educate her on her new role in society.*

*Of course, she realized it would be trial-and-error to learn which activities best suited her. But, at least now she would have new ideas.*

For many older women, becoming single again is a natural outcome of longer life spans, or losing their spouses. On average, women outlive men by seven years. All told, there are nearly 100 million single adults in the United States, according to the latest Census Bureau figures. More than 43% of all Americans are single, with more than 30 million Americans over the age of 55 holding that distinction.

When you're home alone without plans, it gets very lonely. There is no one to plan activities or adventures with. No one to say, "let's go to a movie," or "want to eat out tonight?" There is no reason to even get dressed. Unfortunately, the TV or food or other undermining behaviors are within easy reach. Without question, these new, harmful habits can become debilitating.

If you want to be prepared before your revivement, go to the activity exercise and start discovering your interests. The exercise will help guide you to make choices to get you started on your revivement. Just starting the exercises may lessen your fears about your future.

### Hanna

"As a single woman, I've always been pretty independent. I just took my life's path as normal, and handled the ups and downs myself. I never realized that once I retired, things would be so dramatically different. I would now need to consider how to spend my time—something I had taken for granted because my life was pretty full with my 24/7 job and friends.

"I just didn't know what to expect about retirement," said Hanna. "My parents circumstances were very different. It's a process and everybody is unique. When you think about it, it's like thinking about death, and in

*a way its almost as scary. You know it's coming, and
you can only hope it's good. Friends gave me advice.
Yet, I was skeptical that everything would turn out well.
There is a lot of denial about the reality of retirement,"
she added.*

*Hanna warns that retiring cold turkey can be confusing.
When you lose your routine and don't have someone at
home to challenge your new behavior, you can take a
harmful path. For instance, her friends told her that the
first year she would sleep a lot. "Although I didn't at
first," said Hanna, "I found I was sleeping 12 to 13
hours a day. Is this from being exhausted after years of
working or what? I started having a phone and iPad in
bed, and then sleeping in. My biorhythms got screwed
up for a while." It took Hanna a few months to get her
body and mind back on schedule. It also took determination to not let her life go "down the tubes," she
said. "Here I was with abundant opportunities to enjoy
my life, and I was blowing it."*

*Once Hanna began assessing her revived future, she
realized that there were things she enjoyed about
working. Not everything, but there were enough good
things. If she could just pull them out, she thought she
might find a job or volunteer activity that used her
favorite skills.*

*Hanna finally decided she liked working with people
with similar values and good communication skills, so
she accepted a part-time position where she found both.
Unfortunately, she didn't ask all the questions that
would let her see the bigger picture of her involvement.
This part-time position ended up turning into full-time
work with half-time pay. "I overcommitted and then
realized I didn't have to."*

*After a year, Hanna was able to redesign her job to only work the original 20 hours. Hanna suggests you learn from her lessons to:*

1. *Get a full picture of whatever you want to say "yes" to before you say "yes."*
2. *Make sure you do not overcommit yourself.*
3. *Have an agreement that if the effort begins to take more time than you originally agreed to, that you have the option to either say "no" to additional tasks, or resign without guilt.*
4. *Of course, number 3 above has to be an agreement with yourself as well.*

*Hanna said that being in revivement did give her the opportunity to learn some things she wished she had known, believed, and acted on earlier in her life. First and foremost was to not fear telling the truth to those in power positions. "I did that to avoid risk in my career. I also wish I had asked people with a lot of experience and talent to mentor me, and to realize that I wasn't intruding.*

*"One more thing I hate to admit, and am still learning at my age, is to be able to go out and play when I want to. My parents raised me to believe you don't play until you get your room clean and your work is done. Now, at the age of 70, I'm practicing spontaneity," she added.*

Many single people, responsible for their financial security as well as their emotional well-being, are finding themselves without direction or a plan. If you fit this description, let this book and the worksheets be your friend and your guide to design your future.

No matter your status in life—man, woman, couple, single or otherwise—the bottom line is that you are an individual who needs and wants to take charge of your life. While this chapter describes some ways to help, life is large and there are many options. What's important is that you find what fits for you, make it happen and own it.

So, what do you want to do when you grow up?

How many times in the past have you said, "If I only knew then what I know now. If only I had been smarter, better, and more aware?" Today, those of us over 50 are much more prepared for revivement than our parents. We've come a long way, as we stumbled through our first half of life. All our successes, failures, and life lessons have shaped us. They have filled our personal and professional growth with the expertise we will take into our second half of existence as we redefine and redirect our lives.

In the old paradigm, we might have graduated high school, attended college or a trade school, or gone straight to work. Our mindset was to give our all at a job or career for 30-40 years. The reward at the end of that journey was retirement, and sitting on one's laurels. We don't want that anymore. That was fine when life was shorter, and we didn't understand we would have more time that could be filled with meaningful and enjoyable choices.

**Career**—If there is something you always wanted to do, well, now is the time. Or, if you enjoyed what you were doing, do you want to do it part-time or volunteer in your area of expertise? Or, do you want to try something new? Bounce your ideas off a trusted advisor or good friend.

**People**—What will your relationships be like? Will you join organizations or visit family more often? Our relationships are a key to us becoming who we are. I encourage clients to stay close to family and friends with whom they have good relationships, and foster them.

**Yourself**—Take time to expand yourself personally in whatever way makes sense for you. Have you found the self-regard, self-esteem and self-approval that feels good from the inside out?

By answering these and many more questions in the worksheets in this book, you will form a picture of you and your future. Hopefully, you will have some "aha" moments that you can carry into action and happiness.

## Finding Fulfillment

*"Sometimes it is the artist's task to find out how much music you can still make with what you have left."*

— ITZHAK PERLMAN, *Violinist*

People approach retirement in different ways—sometimes not by their own choice.

### Amy

*Amy's parents taught her that life was about working and bringing home a paycheck, which she did for 30 years. When she was 52, a physical malady required her to retire early. Amy thought, "Now what am I going to do with my time?" She decided to take some art classes.*

*We see Amy in her first sketching class with her pen poised ready to draw. To her amazement, she began to draw beautiful images of animals: a fox, an eagle, a bear, a deer. She said it was as if the images were coming through her. She was both surprised and thrilled! Over time she drew 20 animals, wrote a story about each one, and put all her creations in a book which she bound and gave to her husband for Christmas. He was so proud, he said, "I'm going to get this published."*

*The lesson here is that Amy never knew Amy. In her entire 52 years, she never realized she was a creative and talented artist. Now she will be able to enjoy her new-found innate gifts for the rest of her life. They say don't die with the music still inside you.*

Amy continues to sketch beautiful images. In fact, she won an art contest for an image of a tiger, and loves the validation it gives, although she doesn't expect or need her art to become income-producing. She does it for her own pleasure and to delight others.

She has let her creativity flourish by adding watercolor painting and home decorating to her tool box. Amy is living her dream, while learning to balance other aspects of her life, including time with family and volunteer activities through her service organization.

Here's another example of finding your bliss.

### Carl

*Carl knew what he wanted to do with his life at the age of five. He wanted to be a writer. But like many of us, he found a job, got married, had children, and brought home a paycheck. He took the first job that was offered and worked his way up over a 30-year period from clerk to Vice President of Operations for a manufacturing company. He was good at managing people and organizing projects, so he kept getting promotions and pay raises, but he wasn't happy. "It never felt right," he said. He accomplished the company's goals, "but it wasn't my life's work. I felt like an imposter."*

*When his father died, Carl began to reevaluate his life and his future. He retired at the age of 56, and began to write. It took him six years to hone his craft and to feel he was a competent writer. His first book was picked up by a publisher, and at age 62 he was on his way to fulfilling his dream. Today he has a published book and is working on another. On a side note, I read the first book, and it is good!*

In Part Two, you'll find a series of exercises to help you develop your life plan. It will take you step by step through the nine pillars of a fulfilling life. Once you have your plan, all you have to do is put it into action, and you're on your way. First let's look more closely at what those nine pillars are.

# Chapter Six

*The Pillars of a Fulfilling Revivement*

Revivement is a time to access all that you are to do all that you wish to do with the rest of your years. This works best if you adopt a balanced life. The list below is designed to give you the big picture of your possibilities. You may already have some of these components in place. Or, you may want to look at the following list to make sure you're enjoying all of these gifts. This chapter describes the strong underpinnings of revivement, the pillars that will support you.

## 6-1. Purpose
Purpose is fundamental to your soul. Meaningful work and activity can stimulate an inner core within you that seeks fulfillment.

Here is a nonmedical prescription for having a healthy, long life. Find your purpose! A purpose can direct you to a fulfilling and meaningful life beyond what you may have thought possible. Purpose defines your mission and why you exist, and energizes you to be involved in life. Instead of feeling lost in a world that no longer requires your 24/7-work focus, you have new direction, enthusiasm and involvement.

People who are purposeful have goals, activities, and interests that direct their days and make time on this planet more satisfying. At the same time, they experience the reward of helping others.

Purpose activates our inner talents, skills, and abilities, and we are able to enjoy what we do. There is confirmation that we are expressing ourselves from the inside out—the greatest use of who we are.

Purpose also appears to have a potent ability to improve and extend lives. "It's a very robust predictor of health and wellness in old age," said Patricia Boyle, M.D. a neuro-psychologist at the Rush Alzheimer's Disease Center in Chicago.

Following almost 1,000 people (average age 80) for up to seven years, Dr. Boyle's team found that the ones with "high purpose" scores were 2.4 times more likely to remain free of Alzheimer's than those with low scores. They also were less likely to develop mild cognitive impairment, often a precursor of Alzheimer's. "It slowed the rate of cognitive decline by about 30 percent, which is a lot," Dr. Boyle added.

In addition, her study showed that purposeful people were less likely to develop disabilities or die. A sample of 1,238 subjects followed for up to five years (average age 78) by Rush researchers found that those with high purpose had roughly half the mortality rate of those with low purpose.

## A Reason to Get Up in the Morning
"Okinawans (from Japan) call it 'ikigai' and Nicoyans (from Costa Rica) call it 'plan de vida,' which essentially translates to 'why I wake up in the morning,' writes Dan Buettner in his book *The Blue Zone*. The book describes several cultural

lifestyles in remote areas in the world. The strong sense of purpose posed by elders in these communities, he writes, may act as a buffer against stress and help reduce their chances of suffering from Alzheimer's disease, arthritis, and stroke.

Dr. Robert Butler and his collaborators at the National Institutes of Health studied the correlation between having a strong sense of purpose and longevity. Individuals aged 65 to 92 were followed for 11 years. These older adults expressed a clear goal in life—a reason for getting up in the morning; something that made a difference.

Dr. Mihaly Csikszentmihalyi best describes this feeling in his book, *Flow: The Psychology of Optimal Experience*. He defines flow as a Zen-like state of total oneness with the activity at hand in which you feel fully immersed in what you're doing. It's characterized by a sense of freedom, enjoyment, fulfillment, and skill, and while you're in it, temporal concerns (time, food, ego/self, etc.) are typically ignored.

Personal purpose appears to be a clear path to longevity and a healthy lifespan, as well as happiness and a worthwhile way to live. To find purpose, craft a personal mission statement with the activity guide in this book. Articulate your personal mission by answering this question in a single memorable sentence: "Why do I get up in the morning?" Consider what you're passionate about, how you enjoy using your talents, and what is truly important to you.

## 6-2. Relationships

This is a great playground to help you become you. All your interactions with family, friends, your barber or beautician, coworkers, and other acquaintances have given you a way to test who you are through your communication, behavior, preconditioned responses, bias, and personal style. Like most of us, you may have grown up with a mix of your true self and outside influences. Sometimes you had to fight to be accepted for who you are. In some ways, you may have given up or given in. Today, this is a chance to own who you are, your responses to life, and how you show up in the world.

You succeed in your relationships when you honor individuals for who they are by giving them respect, trust, honesty, and values, and when you use good communication skills. And, with family members and close friends, you share love.

Of course, relationships can sometimes become difficult. Our human failings can bring down the best of relationships unless we monitor ourselves and our actions. That is why you need to have your best relationship with yourself. When you experience self-regard, self-esteem, self-love, and the willingness to grow beyond your comfort levels, you become the best of who you are. I was watching a video in which Melinda Gates shared how she learned to honor who she is. She said she learned that it is so important to become your best integrated self. Then she cited the words of a song she heard by a country western singer in Australia, who sang, "You better be yourself, because everybody else is already taken."

Most of us have had some situations, messages, or other actions occur in our lives that have undermined our true, strong selves. At the time they occurred, we didn't realize that the impact of these false ideas would live with us forever and influence how we related to ourselves. These words, feelings, thoughts and memories still live inside our minds and bodies, and can undermine us. At the same time, as you read earlier, you are in charge of changing those tapes from negative to positive beliefs about yourself to become who you really are.

I speak from personal experience, having changed my
perceptions about myself over the years. I've learned that
some old ideas can pop up unwelcomed, but they are just old
ideas and not who I am.

In case you are struggling with similar self-actualization
issues, do the exercise in the back of the book that will help
you identify where you are with your self-approval. We must
be our best friend and give ourselves the self-acknowledgment
we deserve.

By developing who you are and what you want to do in
your future, you will experience an internal expansion of
possibilities, deepen your interest in life, grow your sense
of self, and become excited about new discoveries. Moreover,
you will look forward to your days with high expectations
of the good things that will unfold.

## Community

*"People, people who need people*
*are the luckiest people in the world."*

—Sung by BARBRA STREISAND, *Singer/Actress*

If you want to extend your life in a happy, healthy, positive way, you need people. The people in your community can be the foundation on which to build a wholesome second half of life as you revive.

In the book *Bowling Alone*, author Robert Putnam said the greatest social epidemic in American life is loneliness. This statement is magnified in revivement for someone who counts on the workplace for socialization. Without other social outlets, this reviver will greatly suffer.

The opposite of loneliness is belonging, and there are so many ways to be part of groups of people that enhance life. As humans we need to belong. It is fundamental to our happiness and sense of life. There are many ways to become part of your community.

If you are sitting on your couch day and night watching television, you are letting the best years of your life fade away. This is the time that you get to do all the great things you always wanted to do. For instance, if you are not now in a variety of social groups, you need to plan to join some. Yes, plan to socialize.

We get a deep look into the importance of community in the book *Tribe: On Homecoming and Belonging* by Sebastian Junger. He writes how tribal societies demonstrate unity and belonging, which are essential to the achievement of meaning and happiness. Junger asserts that while modernity has brought a level of comfort that was unimaginable a thousand years ago, it has done so at the expense of community, freedom, and individual well-being. People can tolerate wars, earthquakes, and other disasters. What they can't stand is feeling inauthentic, unneeded, and unconnected to others.

What makes up a community? It's a group of people living in the same area with shared values, interests, and goals. The feeling "I belong" is evident as one experiences camaraderie and a support system beyond their immediate families. In fact, sometimes your community becomes your extended family.

Community means socialization, safety, and support. The people we connect with usually care about us in a way that helps us feel seen and important. In community we enjoy celebrations and can work together for a greater good. Our lives are more enjoyable when we feel connected to a group that share in our interests and aspirations. In fact, sometimes these people become our friends.

One member of an audience I was speaking to came up to me after the talk and said, "When you were describing how John was lost about what to do with his life after his retirement, you were describing me. Fortunately," he said, "a friend pulled me out of my doldrums and into a few men's organizations. Having those communities have made a huge difference," he said. "My wife even likes me better now."

Having a community of family and friends outweighs financial concerns among older Americans in their later years, according to the second annual United States of Aging Survey. When asked what is most important to maintaining a high quality of life, staying connected to friends and family was a top choice.

For some of us social personalities, choosing new avenues is a little easier than it is for others. We like to go out and meet new people and participate in activities outside our homes. Introverts or shy individuals may find pushing themselves out the door is a little more difficult, but it is important to do so. If you need a little nudge or if you want to go somewhere and/or partake in something new but are hesitant, ask a friend or family member to go with you. Once you are comfortable with your new community, you'll feel like going yourself.

Here are some tips you can pass along to others who need a community, but don't know how to access it or don't feel comfortable joining groups themselves:

1. Ask the person, "What are some things you enjoy that you aren't doing right now?" If that person responds with even one item, you could say, "I know of an organization you might want to explore. I'll go with you to a first meeting if you'd like me to." This way you can encourage that person to connect with those hobbies, organizations, and support groups of interest.

2. Invite the person to go with you to an organization you belong to that you think he/she would enjoy. At the meeting, introduce that person to others whom he may feel comfortable with. Then, ask someone in the organization to sponsor/mentor this person each time they come. Over time as the person becomes more and more comfortable, he/she will be willing to attend without you.

3. Include the person in volunteer activities in which you participate. Giving to others helps us feel better about ourselves. As you know, there are many nonprofit organizations that would appreciate another pair of hands and honed skills to forward their mission.

4. Help that person develop a group of friends based on their own interests. If it's a course at a local college, a group of people engaged in a similar hobby, or any other activity, getting this person started in the right direction will make a big difference in his or her life.

## If You're a Caregiver

Millions of Americans over 50 spend their lives tending to a loved one. Their role of caregiver is often underestimated and misunderstood. It takes enormous energy and selfless behavior to provide 24/7 care. At the same time, caregiving often undermines their health and happiness.

Caregivers often spend hours catering to an aging or ill parent, raising a grandchild, or caring for a disabled sibling, to name a few examples. Although they caretake with love, they often suffer from stress, isolation, exhaustion, and other debilitating illnesses. They can also end up with untold physical, mental, and emotional pain due to the stress of managing someone else's needs as well as their own.

If you take on the role of caretaker at a later age, your physical body no longer has the energy and strength it had when you were younger. You might not have the patience you once did. Whatever the circumstance, taking care of others is exhausting.

Then, there is the money issue. An older couple's retirement funds might not quite be enough for themselves, let alone the expense of hiring a caregiver.

The most important thing you need to do if you have taken on the role of caregiver is to take care of yourself. Remember what the flight attendant tells us as we are taking off in a plane: "If you are traveling with a child and the plane loses oxygen, be sure to put on your oxygen mask first. Then put one on the child." The premise here is that you can't help anyone if you don't help yourself first. Here are some steps you can take to be healthier and happier, and you will be able to do what you need to for the person you take care of.

1. Do not become isolated when caregiving. Get out of the house and socialize with others.

2. If you can afford to, hire caregivers to give you some free time when you are not responsible for anyone but yourself.

3. Don't be codependent. It may be quicker and easier to do a task for a loved one needing help, but it's important for both of you that a sick or disabled person do as much as she/he can.

4. Continue enjoying your own activities. Don't give them up.

5. Keep yourself healthy with nutritious food and exercise.

6. Attain balance, which includes outside interests.

7. Ask for help. Get other family members or friends involved in the caregiving.

8. Schedule yourself a day or two off—totally away from home and caregiving duties.

9. Stay happy. Do things that make you feel good, and do things just for yourself.

## 6-3. Ongoing Learning
Because work is considered part of the revivement lifestyle, some revivers are preparing themselves for new careers, and colleges and universities have developed programs for them that provide knowledge and skill-building.

Another popular revivement option—one I hope is in your plans—is ongoing learning. To me learning is essential as we age. You might want to take classes at the different universities, community colleges, and other study groups that provide this enlightening path.

For instance, many universities are offering educational programs for those over the age of 50. These classes are for individuals who want to learn for the joy of learning while staying in touch with a larger world. Often there is no homework, no tests, or any other requirements. In addition to focusing on the mature adult, educational institutions are also beginning to bring together intergenerational students to learn, work, and socialize together.

As reported in the *New York Times*, deans, provosts, and vice presidents from 22 institutions, including Arizona State University, Columbia University, Community College of Vermont, Cornell University, Denison University, Tulane University, U.C.L.A. and the University of Washington, held a daylong summit at New York University in 2015 to discuss future curriculums and collaborations. The Times noted, "Their mission was to work together on ways to create intergenerational, age-friendly institutions and build a network to help students who want to reboot to service-oriented work."

The Stanford University Distinguished Careers Institute is a dynamic program for established leaders from all walks of life who seek to transform themselves for roles with social impact at local, national, and global levels. In partnership with the Stanford Center on Longevity, this year-long program creates enriching professional and personal pathways for the next stage of life.

In addition to education and new careers, attendees at the 2015 White House Conference on Aging harnessed technology to bring today's conversation about the future of aging to communities across the country. Hundreds of watch parties, where people gather to view a specific event or program together on television, occurred in every state in America, hosted by organizations such as AARP, the National Association of Area Agencies on Aging, Service Employees International Union (SEIU), the Diverse Elders Coalition, Leadership Council of Aging Organization's members, and numerous cities and counties.

Again, this is a tiny sample of the many programs that are growing to address needs of an older population. Find the ones in your community.

### 6-4. Volunteerism

The desire to do good in the world is growing. As baby boomers retire and revive, they have energy, life experience, and professional knowledge to contribute. Because so many nonprofits and charities are in need of help, there's no shortage of volunteer opportunities available for those willing to donate their time and efforts during their revivement.

When individuals get passionate about a cause they want to advance, they become focused, excited, and dedicated. In addition to giving of oneself for the greater good, you will experience an enormous amount of satisfaction. It's the giving and receiving cycle that makes us whole. You also will have opportunities to use or develop skills that you can use in other areas of your life—perhaps in your new work.

*At the age of 40, Charlotte learned she had metastatic melanoma. She was so sure she was going to die that she told her husband to remarry after she was gone. Fortunately, she won her devastating fight with cancer. Ten years later, her husband got pneumonia and almost died. She retired early to be with him. Today, he has recovered and is doing well.*

*When Charlotte retired, she lost her career and income. They had a small farm, so she got involved as a bookkeeper there. Even though she soon realized that the economics of farming hindered the couple's income, that did not stop her from helping others. She welcomed new people to her neighborhood with cookies she baked. She mentored students at the local high school to help them prepare for college. She opened her door and her heart to local people in need and headed up food and clothing collections during the year. Charlotte felt that not dying gave her more reason to help others. "It magnified my heart," she said.*

*"Every day you do the best you can," said Charlotte. "Put yourself in a position where you can support people. You feel a lot of increased personal self-worth, and it helps your perspective of how fortunate you are."*

*If Charlotte could thrive under such daunting circumstances, couldn't she too be an inspiration to the rest of us?*

Some of us find purpose in volunteer projects and are very satisfied. Yet, some of us want to do not only that, but more. We want to find something inside ourselves that has been waiting for the time, the place, and the willingness to appear.

There are many opportunities to volunteer in your local community, but, if your feet are itching to travel, here are a few ideas:

1. A couple, who are friends of mine, recently joined the Peace Corps. They are in their early 60's. They will live and volunteer in a specified area of the world for two-plus years, while making it their temporary home. They are bringing their hearts and skills to a culture that wants to raise its standard of living, for the sake of their children.

2. Some revivers in their 60's, 70's, and 80's volunteer for nonprofits often in exchange for free room and board. They not only save money while volunteering, but they enjoy a deep sense of purpose and adventure in their revivement years. One volunteer group called NOMADS boasts more than 1,000 members across the country. They live in their own RVs. With no mortgage or other debt, their largest expenses include health care, cell phone bills, and fuel for their travels.

3. Many state and national parks offer a variety of volunteer opportunities, with some providing free room and board.

4. Many nonprofits desperately need volunteers. Not all opportunities are advertised. If you have something or somewhere you would love to volunteer that might also accommodate your living conditions and expenses, don't be afraid to ask.

For connection to more organizations, visit websites: www
rotary.org, gatesfoundation.org, VolunteerMatch.org,
allforgood.org and others.

## 6-5. Health/Wellness

Longevity expert Dan Buettner, author of *The Blue Zones* and
*The Blue Zones Solution,* advocates a Mediterranean diet,
taking naps and embracing your community. He says
socializing is key, and that the happiest Americans socialize six
hours a day. This information isn't new, but needs to be
underscored here. This good advice has been ignored in the
past, and needs to be revisited and utilized. Perhaps this story
will give you a good reason why.

A man Buettner interviewed in Ikaria, Greece provides us with
a good example of a longevity lifestyle. His name is Stamatis
Moraitis. At 102, he is famous for partying. Each year he
makes 400 liters [100 gallons] of wine from his vineyards, and
drinks the wine with his friends. His house is the social hot
spot of the island.

He is also the Ikarian who emigrated to the United States, was
diagnosed with lung cancer in his 60s, and given less than a
year to live. He returned to Ikaria to die. Instead, he
recovered. He never went through chemotherapy or treatment.
He just moved back to Ikaria. He returned to the United
States ten years later, to see if the American doctors could
explain why he was still alive. When asked what happened, he
said he never found out because, "my doctors were all dead."

According to the Mayo Clinic, a traditional Mediterranean
diet reduces the risk of heart disease and cardiovascular
mortality as well as overall mortality. The Mediterranean diet
is also associated with a reduced incidence of cancer,
Parkinson's, and Alzheimer's diseases. Women who eat a

Mediterranean diet supplemented with extra-virgin olive oil and mixed nuts may have a reduced risk of breast cancer. For these reasons, most if not all major scientific organizations encourage healthy adults to adapt a style of eating like that of the Mediterranean diet for prevention of major chronic diseases.

Key components of the Mediterranean diet are:
1. Eating primarily plant-based foods, such as fruits and vegetables, whole grains, legumes and nuts

2. Replacing butter with healthy fats such as olive oil and canola oil

3. Using herbs and spices instead of salt to flavor foods

4. Limiting red meat to a few times a month

5. Eating fish and poultry at least twice a week

6. Enjoying meals with family and friends

7. Drinking red wine in moderation (optional)

8. Getting plenty of exercise

Based on current research involving potential therapeutics, Dr. Brian Kennedy of the Buck Institute on Aging in Marin County, California believes that at some point people will eventually be able to get an extra decade of good health. He says new therapeutics will likely be most successful for those who follow the simple basics: eat right, exercise, get a good night's sleep, and have a positive attitude about aging. Other keys to longevity include keeping stress levels low, getting adequate sleep supplemented by daily naps, and enjoying a strong social network of friends and family.

## De-Stress and Treat Your Telomeres with Respect

Stress can be your friend or your enemy over your lifespan. Good stress moves your forward. If you are excited, your pulse quickens and your hormones change, but there is no fear or threat to your person. This good stress, otherwise known as "eustress," is healthy and keeps us feeling alive and happy. A few examples of eustress are getting married, being promoted, or preparing for a vacation. In fact, I am experiencing eustress as I write this book.

On the other hand, bad stress causes untold harm to a human's mind, emotions, and physical body. It's a killer. I don't want to upset you here, but I want to emphasize the importance of taking care of yourself and minimizing stress—especially as you get older.

Bad stress accelerates premature aging and can bring premature death. You've probably noticed that the hair of our U.S. Presidents often turns grey while in office. It's a natural outcome of too much stress and not enough downtime. A man I interviewed for my first book told me, "I was only forty, and my hair was turning gray. Since I've stopped running around in circles for my work, my hair has literally turned brown again."

When stressful challenges occur, your body senses danger and responds by releasing hormones into your bloodstream, which speed up your heart, breathing, and other physical processes and prepare you to react fast to avoid the threat. This natural reaction is known as the stress response. What you want to avoid is chronic stress, which accelerates aging by shortening DNA telomeres.

## What Are Telomeres?

Although the subject of telomeres would have easily fit into Chapter Two where I wrote about emerging research, I placed the topic in this chapter, where I think it is more relevant. Telomeres are best understood as they relate to stress and your lifestyle.

Our bodies are made up of 46 chromosomes, 23 from our mothers and 23 from our fathers. Every chromosome has a protective cap at each end called a telomere. The telomere's job is to protect how our body functions within its particular sphere of influence. Healthy telomeres retain their length, and therefore keep stored all the files we've accumulated over our lifetime. But, as telomeres become shorter, often due to stress, their structural integrity weakens. The cells can no long divide or replenish themselves. This causes cells to age faster and die younger, resulting in chronic diseases and premature death. A study published in the Proceedings of the National Academy of Sciences confirms this outcome. Over our lifetime, telomeres naturally become shorter as a key process of aging and one of the reasons humans can't live forever. Yet, we can delay their decline by avoiding harmful stress.

A wide range of studies have shown that the stress caused by things like untreated depression, social isolation, long-term unemployment, anxiety attacks and other harmful events can speed up the aging process by shortening the length of each DNA strand. Research also shows that long-term activation of your body's stress response impairs your immune system's ability to fight against disease and increases the risk of physical and mental health problems. For example, studies have shown that stress and anxiety in older adults are associated with the following:

- Increased physical problems, such as disability and difficulty in carrying out activities of daily living

- Increased health problems, such as coronary artery disease

- Decreased sense of well-being and satisfaction with life

Here's the good news. If you experience negative stress, your body is telling you to pay attention and make necessary changes that will restore your health. This is doable. Science has proven that by taking the right actions, you can decrease your negative stress and extend your life.

**Maintaining a positive outlook** is one key—a study by Yale University found that people who feel good about themselves as they get older live about seven and a half years longer than "glass half empty" types. Researchers say people with more positive attitudes may also deal with stress better and have a stronger will to live. Staying close to friends and family is an excellent way to cut down on stress. As reported by the American Psychological Association, social support can help prevent stress and stress-related diseases.

**The benefits of friends and family** can be especially striking for older individuals. An article published in the *American Journal of Health Promotion* notes that social support can slow down the flow of stress hormones in agers and, not coincidentally, increase longevity. Other studies have found that social interactions can help older people stay mentally sharp and may reduce the risk of Alzheimer's.

**Exercise** is a proven stress-buster for people of all ages, and may be especially valuable in later years. Regular walks, bike rides, yoga, or water aerobics can do more than keep a person strong and independent; exercise can actually help block the effects of aging on cortisol levels.

Cortisol is a life-sustaining adrenal hormone essential to the maintenance of homeostasis. It is a natural and protective response to a perceived threat or danger. Called "the stress hormone," cortisol influences, regulates or modulates many of the changes that occur in the body in response to stress.

**Eating a well-balanced diet and getting a good night's sleep** are major contributors to your health.

## Socialize

Find ways to be with people who you enjoy as often as you can. Look at your local community colleges and recreation centers for the many activities they offer such as a bridge group, volunteering, hiking, art classes. Take a tai chi class to use this form of martial arts as a way to relieve stress.

In the end, anything that reduces unnecessary stress will make the later years more enjoyable. Some people simply need to stop trying to do too many things at once. Others may want to try breathing exercises or other relaxation techniques. Still others may need to talk to a psychologist or other therapist to find a new perspective on their lives.

Whatever the approach, fighting stress overload is worth the effort. The American Psychological Association reports that reducing stress in later years can help prevent disabilities and trips to the hospital. And if you end up feeling younger, healthier, and happier, then kudos. You've taken control of your life by taking control of your health.

## Signs of Stress

Age does not define all of our aches and pains. Your body can respond to external factors based on how you react to life stresses. Negative stress is often the culprit when you have one or more of the following symptoms:

- Worry, anxiety, or panic attacks
- Sadness or depression
- Feeling pressured and hurried
- Irritability and mood swings
- Difficulty concentrating and making decisions/memory issues/forgetfulness
- Physical symptoms, such as stomach problems, headaches, or chest pain
- Allergic reactions, such as a skin rash or asthma
- Problems sleeping
- Feeling overwhelmed and helpless
- Drinking too much alcohol, smoking, or misusing drugs
- Change in eating habits: overeating/ loss of appetite
- Sexual dysfunction

Please pay attention to these warning signs. Get a checkup and some advice from your doctor on how to change the negative impact of stressors in your life.

## Balance

Balance is an essential part of a healthy life. It is the perfect harmony of all the elements—mental, physical, emotional and spiritual-- that keeps you engaged, happy and not stressed. You are integrated. You can embrace the fullness of who you are. The consequences of being out of balance can be seen by what happens, for instance, if you work too much. That leads to stress, which can cause illness. After retirement, too little structure and social activity can lead to depression, which can also cause illness.

If you are still working as you prepare to retire, how do you bring balance into your life when your job requires so much focus and time? Can you be successful at work and still have a life? How will incorporating life-work balance into your days now support you when you are in revivement? If you are already in revivement, what are you doing today to integrate these important parts of you?

*Doris Kearns Goodwin, a historian, biographer, and author of books about several American presidents, addressed this vital topic. She told of the seminar led by renowned psychologist Erik Erikson she attended at Harvard University as a young student. She said, "He taught that the richest and fullest lives attempt to achieve an inner balance between three realms: work, love and play; and to pursue one realm with disregard to the others is to open oneself to ultimate sadness in older age. But, to pursue all three with equal dedication, is to make a life possible not only with achievement but with serenity."*

*When speaking, Goodwin noted Lincoln's balance, brought about through the enjoyment of his many interests, as well as his humor, devotion to family, and dedication to work. She contrasted Lincoln to Lyndon Johnson, whose imbalance was due to the exclusive and narrow career path he traveled. Once retired, Johnson, she said, was never able to enjoy life.*

These are strong thoughts that need to be absorbed by today's 24/7 work-oriented individuals. By enjoying the fullness of life now—which includes your work, relationships, health/vitality, volunteerism, ongoing learning, spirit, and leisure—you will know how to enjoy your future.

The Mayo Clinic staff asks us to consider the consequences of poor work-life balance by providing this list:

1. **Fatigue.** When you're tired, your ability to work productively and think clearly might suffer—which could take a toll on your professional reputation or lead to dangerous or costly mistakes.

2. **Poor health.** Stress is associated with adverse effects on the immune system and can worsen the symptoms you experience from any medical condition. Stress also puts you at risk for substance abuse.

3. **Lost time** with friends and loved ones. If you're working too much, you might miss important family events or milestones. This can leave you feeling left out and might harm relationships with your loved ones. It's also difficult to nurture friendships if you're always working.

4. **Increased expectations.** If you regularly work extra hours, you might be given more responsibility—which could lead to additional concerns and challenges.

Here are some tips to help you restore your equilibrium:

1. Figure out what's important. Stop and make a list of what's important to you and how it will increase your happiness, sense of self, involvement in your world, and success.

2. Add goals, dates, and outcomes to achieve to your list.

3. Really do it. Actualize your list by activating it now. Don't wait another day.

4. Health is number one. Take care of your health by getting essential sleep, learning to say no, and not working 24/7. Consider 8/5.

5. Unfocus from work when you leave for the day and refocus on your life. Leave work at work most of the time. Understandably there are a few projects that need more time, but minimize them.

6. Use technology instead of letting it use you. Plan how to interact with technology so you're in charge and not usurped by responding to other people's messages. If you feel you always need to respond, then just turn the device off.

7. Take a break. Take a mindful rest period to revitalize your brain and energy during the day.

By taking care of you, you will improve how you take care of your business commitments. The work will get done, and you'll also have a life. Then, when you transition to revivement, your life will already be full, and this change won't seem as traumatic as it can be. As a reviver, you will have the advantage of embodying this new stage of life with aplomb. After all, you earned it.

## 6-6. Spirit

Following a spiritual path has different meanings for individuals. For some it means practicing specific spiritual principles, for some it is the connection to a religion, for others it's about finding beauty and awe in everyday life and your surroundings or twinkling back at the stars, appreciating someone's smile, or finding peace through mindfulness and meditation. There are so many ways to connect with your spirituality. You probably practice some of the principles without giving them a name.

The world's major religions and spiritual practices agree on the universal truths that speak to mankind's deepest values. People who seek a peaceful and rewarding life follow those principles that align with their beliefs. Here are a list of tenets to stimulate your thinking:

1. Expressing gratitude for all the good from the time you wake until you close your eyes to sleep at night.

2. Living with integrity. Honoring yourself and others by being your true self everywhere you walk in life.

3. Giving of yourself to those in need, and giving to those who don't know they need by sharing your experience and knowledge.

4. Being mindful of the present moment by being aware.

5. Encouraging nonviolence and acceptance of differences between yourself and others.

6. Practicing the Golden Rule by treating others as you wish to be treated.

7. Extending good will and practicing right action.

8. Expressing hope and belief in the future.

9. Realizing that everything is connected, and that you are not truly separate from others.

10. Having genuine compassion for yourself and others.

This list is not finite. Use it to think about what you want your spiritual life to provide to and through you. Add concepts that fit your beliefs.

## 6-7. Leisure

Leisure is the freedom to use your time for mere enjoyment. It certainly needs to be part of your lifestyle design. You no longer "have to" do anything. You can experience pleasure and bask in the glory of your favorite activities. If you want to travel, then travel! Play golf, play! Learn a musical instrument or act in a theater production. Do it! In other words, you pick and choose from the list of hundreds of possible pleasures and make them real.

If you always hoped to strive for life balance, now is the time. But, be aware, all pleasure and nothing else is not balance.

By following your dreams, you also may find yourself on a lifetime adventure you didn't expect, but love. In fact, it may embody you to take your life in a completely new direction.

### *Lorraine*

*Lorraine, 52, was Ms. Corporate America. She wore business suits, maintained a busy schedule, and kept up with her contacts as a super saleswoman. She was good at her job and earned six figures, so she stuck with it. Her work was stressful. The bosses, the rules, pushing to make sales goals—the whole thing was wearing.*

*When she found out she could get an early retirement package, she quit, even though she had to hang onto her job another year to get it. And, she did, frustrated and complaining all the way. It was worth the wait. That was ten years ago.*

*After she left her company, all she knew is that she had always wanted to travel. Maybe she could lead tours.*

*Maybe she would become a travel agent. She wasn't sure. Of course, never having traveled very much, she realized she needed to test out these possibilities, so she and her husband set off on their first trip to hang out in Asia and Africa for six months. Since they started, they've explored other parts of the world for months at a time, always staying in low cost accommodations and shifting their schedules to meet changing weather and social conditions.*

*What they've found is a lifestyle that suits them. They pick a location, make a few plans, and get on a plane. Most of what they do is literally hang out and let life happen. In this way they have had fascinating experiences. They've met people from diverse cultures and participated in cultural events. They've seen vistas, oceans, mountains, cities, and rain forests. They are truly world travelers.*

*In this walk of life they not only have gained a broader perspective of people and the world, but have grown deeper and more knowing inside themselves. During her revivement, this driven corporate lady let go of her exterior and found her true soul.*

## 6-8 Lifestyle

Do you want to move or revive in place? A major aspect of revivement planning involves the decision of where to live. Today many revivers are moving closer to their adult children to maintain their relationships. They are also moving into communities where they can make new friends and be socially and intellectually stimulated.

## Alice and Eric

*Alice and Eric started thinking about their revivement prior to her leaving her job of 25 years. She had held an Executive Director position in a major financial corporation, and oversaw 102 employees. The adjustment for her was going to be major.*

*Alice's initial concern about revivement was her apprehension about the unknown. When you've been deeply involved in your career, it's a huge part of your identity. "Everything revolved around my job, even though there are other things going on in my life," she said.*

*Her husband, Eric, on the other hand, had always run his consulting business out of their home, so he understood the feast and famine of entrepreneurial life and was able to adjust to changes more easily. When the downturn in the economy hit in 2008, he said "I'm done!" He stopped working and continued to enjoy his outside activities and interests.*

*The couple had "flirted" with the idea of buying a home in a senior retirement community that offered amenities and activities. They spent weekends traveling up and down the West coast visiting potential sites. Within five months after retiring they bought a home at Leisure Life, an over-55 community. But they still weren't sure if they wanted to revive in place—spend their second half of life in their present home and community—or sell their home and move. "I still had friends and a home that I had been in for 25 years," said Alice. So, they decided to rent out their Leisure Life home until they were sure.*

*After a year and much debating, Eric and Alice decided to make the big move. "We had purchased this lovely home that met our needs and desires," said Alice. "We needed to give it a try.*

*"I found that the new community opened up a whole new world for me to explore. As I began to investigate my new outer world, I was reexamining my inner world as well."*

*Over time, Alice let go of the identity she had in her professional life. She said she now lives in a community that doesn't care about what you've done or where you've been. She is more focused on the present.*

*Eric and Alice have found a balance of new interests, pursuits and involvement in their new community. "It's part of my makeup to want to make an impact and contribute my skills, and I'm able to do that by membership on a Board that serves the older adult population at Leisure Life," she added.*

*Alice also started classes in tap dancing, art appreciation, and memoir writing. The transition allowed her to honor this part of her life by doing things she never allowed herself to do when she was working.*

*While it took Alice a total of three years to ease into revivement, now when Eric says, "Let's go to the movies, we can go during the day," Alice answers, "We still don't do that much. We are often too busy doing other things."*

*"One of the big transition pieces, which is sometimes challenging, is that it's up to you to schedule life now. There is discomfort and anxiety in having all that free time and in having to make choices. Alice has mastered that concern. "Today, instead of worrying and fretting about free time, I embrace my life as it is."*

One lesson you can learn from Alice and Eric is not to sell your present home until you know for sure that your new residence and community are a fit. I've seen too many people move to what they assume will be a wonderful new location, only to miss their friends, family, and former community groups. My recommendation is that once you find a new area, test it out. Rent a home in that area and rent out your present home. That way, if things don't turn out as you had hoped, you can always come back to the community you know and love. If you sell your home and want to return, you might not be able to afford a home in your former hometown.

### Jake and Sarah

*Jake and Sarah discovered this lesson too late. Hawaii seemed beautiful and affordable when they explored the island as a potential retirement site. While searching for a house, they spent weeks at a time living in the area. They even met some nice people and began to socialize. Feeling they had done their homework, they sold their home in California, and left the community they had enjoyed for close to 20 years. Although they appreciated the lifestyle and moderate temperatures of Hawaii, the couple annually returned to their hometown because they missed their closest friends and family. "We realized that although we come back here once a year to see everyone, that isn't enough. As we get older, we want to be with our closest friends more often and we want to see our grandchildren grow up," said Sarah. "The problem now is we can't find an affordable home. When we sold our home, the market was down. Now the market is high. We're not sure what to do."*

A more successful example is Gina, a single woman in her 60's.

## Gina

*Gina wanted to pump some new energy into her life. She thought it would be fun to move out West—new places to explore, new people to meet, and perhaps she might even meet her life partner. Fortunately, she listened to her financial adviser and rented out her home before pulling up stakes permanently. Gina rented a condo in Denver, and was so glad she did. When her dreams of adventure didn't turnout the way she had hoped, she was able to move back to her original home. Still itching to find new adventures and another place to explore, Gina moved to Reno, Nevada which was also near her family. Again, she rented out her primary home. Now that she is finally happy with her new location, she says she might sell her house or she might keep it as a rental for income.*

## Other Housing Models

There are a plethora of housing communities with built-in social opportunities and activities to consider, especially if you decide to downsize and live more or less independently. They include eco-villages, over-age-55 communities, cohousing, residential land trusts, income-sharing communes, student co-ops, spiritual communities, and other residential properties where people live together on the basis of common values.

For example, in cohousing, future residents may be involved in the design of the housing units to encourage a sense of community. Common supplemental facilities are designed for daily use. The community area includes a common kitchen, dining area, sitting area, children's playroom, and laundry, and also may contain a workshop, library, exercise room, crafts room, and/or one or two guest rooms. Residents manage their own cohousing communities and also perform much of the work required to maintain the property. They participate in the preparation of common meals and meet regularly to solve problems and develop policies for the community.

Another model of home sharing that some revivers enjoy is when a homeowner offers accommodations in exchange for an agreed level of support in the form of financial exchange, assistance with household tasks, or both. An owner who wants to share her home might be an older citizen, a person with disabilities, a working professional, someone at-risk of homelessness, a single parent, or simply a person wishing to share his or her life and home with others. The community is also a beneficiary of home sharing. Shared living makes efficient use of existing housing, helps preserve the fabric of the neighborhood, and, in certain cases, helps to lessen the need for costly chore/care services and long-term institutional care in addition to offering companionship, affordable housing, security, and mutual support.

The National Shared Housing Resource Center (NSHRC) provides information to consumers and organizations who want to learn more about shared housing programs in their community. NSHRC's directory page on their website lists shared housing programs and Regional Coordinator information throughout the country as well as a link to International Shared Housing programs. For more information, visit www.nationalsharedhousing.org.

Retirement communities, cohousing, and other shared housing options aren't for everyone. Very independent revivers want to live in their own homes on their own terms forever. Even if they no longer can navigate their everyday lives, they are determined to make their autonomy work. Fortunately, many communities are devising voluntary programs for older residents that they can access by calling a phone number. For instance, The Village to Village Network is located in some communities nationwide, and these communities are growing. This non-profit, volunteer-supported, membership organization seeks to address the service gap that many face and strives to help older individuals age in place safely, confidently, and independently. They provide vetted volunteers who assist with local rides, household help, pet care, tech support, office organization, companionship, and more. Find them on their website: http://vtvnetwork.org/.

### 6-9. Finances

Today most revivers fear outliving their finances. After all, when and if they started saving and investing 20-40 years ago, the dollar was worth a lot more. Even pensions from before and after the year 2000 don't measure up to a living wage today. The American Institute of Economic Research reports that the cost of living has increased by 184% since 1985. In other words, the dollar in 1985 was worth 54 cents in 2015. Because of the blessing of longevity, older adults are worried about losing their homes and lifestyles. What a conundrum to face at this best time of life.

If you are a couple, finances and how you handle them can be a big area of disagreement. When you head for revivement, you need to add this piece to your conversation so that both parties understand how you will move forward on finances together. The big word here is compromise. As difficult as it might be, always put in front of you what you value most. If it's your relationship, then find ways that you both can win at how you handle your finances.

## Liz

*"I had huge fears that I would end up being a bag lady under the bridge," Liz said, stating a fear many single and married women have today. "Although I have extensive financial acumen and business experience, I haven't kept track of our finances. My husband did. I put my head in the ground—the ostrich thing."*

*When Liz realized that she needed to understand the bigger picture of her new revived life, which included finances, she and her husband went to their financial adviser to get an update. "It was reassuring that we were going to be okay. This was at the bottom of the financial crisis. What I didn't realize is that where we were starting from had nowhere to go but up. At first, it was a little scary.*

*"One of the most helpful things the financial planner told us was to see our first 10 years after revivement as go-go, and next ten as the go-slow years. Go-go while*

*your body can do it—travel, ski, and all the physical things. Then, you'll be ready to slow down when your body does. A side benefit of slowing down is that your expenses do, too."*

Single women who have relied on one salary, who now will have one pension and one Social Security check, need to also focus on their finances with a financial advisor to help them strategize how to keep their income growing.

There are many ways, in addition to going back to work, that can punch up your income. Here are a few more recent options to also consider. One caveat. I am not an expert in this area and therefore I'm just providing information to help stimulate your ideas. I suggest you flush out your options by researching new advances as they become available. Again, ask vetted experts in the financial, insurance, and real estate professions to guide you.

What can we do today to keep ourselves housed, fed, and enjoying life for 30 or more years? Here are three new ideas to stimulate your thinking about adding income to your coffer. Ask experts about these and more options so that you make good choices.

### Idea One. Reverse Mortgages

A reverse mortgage, or home equity conversion mortgage, is a special type of home loan that lets you convert a portion of the equity in your owned home into cash. If you are 62 or older, you can get a lump sum or receive monthly installments. In other words, based on the amount of equity you have accrued, you can receive a monthly check that supplements your present income. This transaction must be set up with a qualified mortgage lender.

157

The owner does not have to make any mortgage payments back to the bank until he/she leaves the property or the home is sold. The borrower must continue to pay property taxes and homeowners insurance and maintain the home. It's important to note that the mortgage must be paid back when the borrower no longer occupies the home as a primary residence.

Reverse mortgages are often considered a last-resort source of income, but they have become a great planning tool for homeowners who need peace of mind from supplemental income. Make sure you have a good financial advisor who will tell you if this is a good strategy for you before you take any steps in this direction.

### Idea Two. Airbnb

Another option is to set up part of your home as an Airbnb. One retiree told me she is happily taking advantage of this new trend, renting out part of her home to interesting travelers from a variety of countries. Now in her late 70's, she shares the concern with many older adults that she might not make it financially during her final years. Instead, she collects rents from vacationers and stacks the money away in growth funds she chooses based on advice she receives from her financial planner. She says she feels more in charge of her future and is saving for her "old age."

### Idea Three. Lilypad Homes

Let's say you have a large part or all of your mortgage paid off, don't wish to put your assets into buying a new home, and don't really want to move. But, in truth, you also don't really need all that space anymore. Lilypad Homes is a nonprofit organization that helps homeowners create totally private in-law apartments from spare space in their homes to rent out for supplemental income.

Rachel F. Ginis, the Executive Director, is a Leadership in Energy and Environmental Design (LEED) accredited residential designer and general contractor. She developed a model for flexible infill housing—building housing in an established community—that she promotes and helps to advance through Lilypad. She told me she created the idea when, as a single working mom, she needed to find a way to earn additional income that would allow her to stay in her home. She did this by turning her master bedroom into a lovely little apartment, known as a junior accessory dwelling unit (JADU) in local permitting code, which she continues to rent. Her personal experience led her to realize that she had developed an innovative model for flexible housing that others could use to remain in their homes. She worked to pass the new code in many cities in Marin County in California, and worked with utility agencies to eliminate fees for these units. This ultimately led to passing a state law that makes the re-purposing of spare bedrooms into flexible units easy and inexpensive to do.

Ginis is now focused on getting jurisdictions to pass the ordinance in California and creating financing sources that allow homeowners to make this transition in the way they are living in their homes, building in privacy and a secure source of income. The organization also works directly with homeowners to develop ADUs (accessory dwelling units) and JADUs in the Bay Area. She expects one day this model will be utilized nationwide, as there are similar housing patterns throughout the United States.

## How to Prepare Yourself to Stay on Top of Your Finances

*"Money is a great servant and a bad master."*
— FRANCIS BACON, *English Philosopher,*
*Statesman and Scientist*

Most of us are not financially prepared to sail into our later years worry-free. We see that we might outlast our financial resources, and we fear becoming destitute.

Unfortunately, we forget that money is just a facilitator. It is a means of bartering to get what we want. You tell me an item is $25, and if I give you $25 you'll give me the item. In a way, it's that simple.

Money is not the owner of our souls, hearts, ideas, or relationships. We are! Yet, because we've been socialized to give money power, it often runs our lives. Sometimes we spend our years as slaves to money, when instead we need to take charge. We need to make our money work for us.

Wherever you are today in your financial life, decide to make it work for you. Find out what you'll need to get you by into your older age. Think, what if you live to 100 or 110. How much can you draw on to be comfortable?

Use some of the ideas below, add your own, and personalize your new relationship with the money you can actually have for the rest of your life.

Begin now to structure your finances to last until you are at least 107.

## The Five R's

Our world economy is based on financial incentives. We sell our services, products, and ideas, and we get paid an agreed-upon price. We want to buy a house, a car, and a million other things, so we pay for them.

Some of you have stayed on top of this game, and are doing well financially. But if you are like me—yes I include myself— and are at a point in life where you want to do a better job, you can start now. Here are some ways to help you start taking back your power by using the next steps to take control of your finances.

### Rethink Your Finances

Don't live in fear. Get perspective. You've come a long way— make a list of all of your wins and successes. See on paper how you navigated your life landscape and arrived at your home port unscathed. Oh, maybe a few scratches here and there, but mostly you are okay. If you got here, you can accomplish the next steps to protect your future.

Now, put on your positive mindset, and understand that you don't have to be controlled by your finances anymore. You can be in control. You might need to change your relationship with money, or change how you interact with money, so start doing things that will get you further along the road to your goals.

Further your financial education by taking classes, or get coaching from a financial advisor.

When you know what you need to do, start new money habits that will positively help you grow your income, savings, and investments.

## Repair When Needed

How have you dealt with your finances? Have you saved and invested? Or are you living month to month? Or, like many of us, did you do all the right things, only to lose it all when the economy went flat in 2008?

What's important here is not to stand in the muddle of what was, but get into what can be possible. What can you do now to start again? Remember, you still have many years ahead of you. You can catch up.

## Revitalize

Find a financial advisor (certified financial planner/advisor) or other professionally proven person or group that you trust to help you structure your financial present and future. Look for someone who looks at your life, not just your assets.

Become financially literate by reading books and articles that educate you.

Understand your personal finances and how to maximize their growth or minimize the risks. Plan your future in concert with planning your finances.

If you have an IRA, determine optimal withdrawal rates and timing, taking into account such factors as longevity, inflation, taxes, market conditions and future health care and housing needs.

If you are married, make sure you are mostly aligned with where you are and where you both want to be. It helps tremendously when you have common goals and can work on this together.

## Reinvent

What you do now regarding your finances will support the rest of your life. This is no longer just about retirement and pensions and Social Security. Think bigger and bolder. How can you supplement what you have now? Do you intend to work? Or, do you have other income potential from products, services, websites, inventions, artistic endeavors, or other talents?

Amazing income streams occur when we follow our bliss. I know of a photographer who, by accident, learned to use her iPhone to take professional photos. Today, she turns them into pieces of saleable art. And they are beautiful. In other words, can you monetize what you love to do and turn it into an income stream?

## Reinvest

Once you have money flow, systematically put a percentage of your new income into a solid investment, a bank account, a money market account or another type of growth opportunity. Choose wisely and understand how your money can grow. You need patience, purpose and planning for this part.

This is just the tip of the reinvention iceberg. Sit down with a financial professional you trust and get guidance in this very important aspect of your future.

## How Employers Can Help

Innovative employers are catching on as well. They are developing new programs to address the growing numbers of Baby Boomers, and help their employees answer questions such as, "What happens to our lives and finances after we retire? What if we still want to work? Is there value in aging us out or keeping us?"

In a recent Towers Watson survey of 457 U.S. large and mid-size employers with retirement plans, 84 percent of the firms said they expect to increase efforts to educate employees on saving and investing over the next two or three years. Company policy decisions about retirement age and re-employment are also being considered.

"For most Baby Boomers, retirement is no longer a point in time at which one immediately stops working," said Catherine Collinson, president of the Transamerica Center for Retirement Studies. "This cannot be accomplished without employers having programs and employment practices in place to facilitate it," said Collinson.

At the same time, Steve Ulian, managing director for institutional retirement and benefit services at Bank of America Merrill Lynch says, "Employers are convinced they need to do more to help employees achieve successful retirements. This help goes far beyond increasing their match for 401(k) contributions or finding investment options with lower fees." It involves what he calls a "sea change" in employers' willingness to provide lifestyle and broad financial advice. "Employees — there's no other way to put this — are crying out for help," Ulian says.

## Other Tips
### Survivors' Benefits
If your major income earner (spouse/partner/parent) predeceases you, there are a host of things you'll need to address—housing, lifestyle, family, and more. While it may be challenging to think about finances at this time, it's important to do so. Check out your benefits at www.socialsecurity.gov to learn about survivor's benefits.

### Delay Claiming Your Own Social Security
You can start claiming your Social Security at age 62, but by

starting early, you future checks will be smaller for the rest of your life. If you wait until you are Full Retirement Age (FRA), you will get 100% of your benefits. And if you wait until you are 70, your checks will be even larger. If you've been married ten or more years to a spouse who pre-deceases you, you can claim your spouse's Social Security at age 60 and delay yours until you are 70. You can find out your personal Social Security information and receive guidance by visiting your local Social Security office.

### The Social Security System Will Exist

My research tells me that the Social Security system is not going defunct. Although coffers will be exhausted by 2033 if funding and benefit levels stay as they are, the program could still pay 75 percent of scheduled benefits even without a fresh infusion of taxes, according to a Social Security Trustee's report.

At the same time, do what you can to get your finances in order. It might mean cutting a lot of things out for a while. But, once you do, you will regain control.

### Documents Vital to Your Future

Develop a realistic long-term-care plan even if you are healthy. If you need care, decide who will provide it and how it will be paid. Put it in writing through a written health directive.

Be sure all important papers/documents are in order – your will, living trust, beneficiary designations, etc.—and that a loved one or designated executor with your power of attorney knows where they are kept. Detail your expectations and indicate if you need care, who will provide it and how will it be paid. Make clear your arrangements for end of life decisions. Defining your expectations makes it easier on those who will be following your wishes. And you will find peace in knowing that your wishes will be honored.

# Chapter
# Seven

*The Legacy Loop*

*Wherever I go meeting the public… spreading a message*
*of human values, spreading a message of harmony, is the most*
*important thing.*

— Dalai Lama

As the age of wisdom approaches, many of us realize we want to share our values and hard-earned lessons with younger generations. After all, they don't have to learn everything the hard way.

My 23-year-old granddaughter and I were talking one day about values. I mentioned that she had interviewed me on that topic for her high school homework assignment when she was a sophomore. She didn't remember.

Fortunately, I kept my copy of those answers (and the answers that I gave to other grandchildren who had similar assignments) on my computer. I was able to retrieve them to share back with her. She read the copy with new eyes and older thinking.

I was glad I had saved them. Here are some of my values that I passed along to her based on the questions from her assignment. I have also added questions from another granddaughter's assignment.

I suggest you look at your list of values from the exercise in the back of the book, and then read my responses below. Pull together a list that is meaningful to you. Then you can choose who to share it with—your spouse, partner, children, grandchildren or others.

## My Legacy/My Values

Here are the questions and my responses to my granddaughters' assignments:

**1. What career advice can you give me?**
Do what you love. Use your skills and talents that give you joy. Get any training, coaching or classes that will help you grow your skills. Find people who do what you want to do and ask them to mentor you. For instance, if you want to be a clothing designer, meet someone who can tell you what you need to do to become one.

**2. What advice about life can you share with me?**
Know yourself. Be true to who you are and your values. Don't let anyone undermine you. Be independent in your actions. Don't look to others for acceptance; rather, keep your sense of self by knowing you are doing the right things. Recognize your talents and skills and grow them with practice. Become strong and resilient, because life will throw some lemons at you, and you need to learn how to turn them into lemonade.

**3. What is the best way to deal with disappointment?**
Learn from it. Every disappointment gives us an important lesson. Learn the lesson so you don't have to repeat the disappointment. Life keeps giving us opportunities to learn when we don't pay attention. Also, think of the positive side. Step outside of yourself and see the disappointment from a different angle. Sometimes it is good to ask someone who

cares about you (family or friends) what they see. Then you make a decision about what to do.

## 4. What can you tell me about dealing with low self-esteem?

It undermines you. A person assumes she has no self-worth, when she actually has tremendous self-worth. Just look at all the things you have accomplished so far in your life. Think of all the opportunities life will give you to grow. Don't worry about what others think. The truth is they are too busy worrying about themselves and don't have that much time to think about you. People who need to put others down are trying to feel better about themselves but are actually making themselves weak. Just know the good in yourself and do your best every day. Most of all, love yourself. Self-love is key to high self-esteem.

## 5. Who do you suggest as people to admire?

Certainly NOT movie stars and singers whom you hardly know. You can admire their talent, but you don't know them personally. Instead, admire those who show their personal values and strength by their actions. People who do good for others. People who treat others with respect and kindness. People who keep their promises. People who overcome difficulties and turn around and do good.

## 6. When is the most important time in life?

Every day of your life is important. Each day brings you something new to learn from and grow on. Important times are when you understand the lessons life gives you and incorporate them into your life.

### 7. What advice would you give a young adult who is unsure of a direction?

To ask the right people for advice, but then make up your own mind. Do your research. Seek information from friends, adults, online, or other groups. There are also counselors at school and organizations that specialize in areas you might be interested in. Get a mentor. Also, if you are unsure, try something. If it doesn't feel right, you can always change direction.

### 8. What qualities make a person successful in life?

Living your life purpose and personal mission. Having a good attitude and being willing to work toward a successful final outcome. Understanding that we learn from our mistakes. See failures as tools toward your personal growth and don't get down on yourself, but find solutions and move forward. Being a successful person means willingness to give of yourself, use your skills and talents, and create from your core.

### 9. What qualities make a person a good person?

Integrity, truthfulness, caring about others, giving of oneself for the greater good, being responsible for one's own life and supportive of others, being fair to all concerned. Having a good set of values and a good moral code.

### 10. Are there any absolute or objective standards of right and wrong? If so, what are they?

Right is when you travel the higher road. When you live your life based on good values. Wrong is when you hurt others both emotionally and physically, steal from, or embarrass, make fun of, or undermine others.

### 11. Overall, what advice would you give to me about life?

How I should live—my future, career, investments,

technology, national politics, global politics, marriage
and family?

Learn, learn, learn about any endeavor you want to
undertake. Learn about life. Again, make sure what you do is
in keeping with solid values. Show respect. Be kind. Be fair. Be
honest with yourself and others. Never stop learning. And,
remember to always value yourself.

## 12. How would you define happiness?

Happiness comes from within. It's a sense of satisfaction one
feels when you are aligned with your personal truth, honor
who you are, and are living on purpose.

## 13. At this point, what is the highest priority of your life?

For me, it's living my personal purpose and my mission
through my work by empowering others to live a fulfilling
and meaningful life.

## 14. If someone asked you to explain your philosophy of life (the ideals you live by), what would you say? What reasons would you give to justify your answer?

My personal philosophy is to use all of the above
explanations and live by my moral code, help others and be
of service to the greater good. Also, live openly and honestly.
I do so because I feel it is right, and because it feels right it
brings me peace within myself.

## 15. What is your view concerning the existence of God, or the nature of ultimate reality? What reasons would you give to justify your answer?

I believe deeply in God and the blessings of the greater
Universe to guide and support me through my life. It is an
inner belief that is part of my truth. There is no justification.
I just believe.

## 16. In your view, what are the most basic or fundamental human problems?

Greed, selfishness, unwillingness to look at how one negatively impacts others, inability to learn from failure and move on, lack of good attitude and seeing the good in others. Also, taking one's anger and pain out on others.

## 17. Is there a solution to the most basic human problems? If so, what is it?

Education is key as is modeling the behaviors we want others to use, eliminating destructive behaviors and substance abuse, eliminating physical and emotional abuse.

## 18. What qualities do you think best suit a mentor?

A mentor needs to be knowledgeable, experienced, a good teacher, positive and honest. He or she gives praise but also constructive advice, provides good guidance to information

and actions that will help you advance, is accessible and supportive. You also need to know how to treat a mentor. Respect his/her contribution and the time given you. Show appreciation.

### 19. What question do you most wish you could answer in your life?

Will the path I'm on make a difference in the lives of others?

Use the exercise sheets in the back of this book to develop your answers to these important life questions. You'll find that you then have a road map for the rest of your life.

My values are important to me, and I want to leave them as a guide to my family. What legacy are you leaving your family?

### Leave the World a Better Place

ˆI also want to leave the world a better place. Are you interested in making an impact in the world? Have you considered what kind of world your children and grandchildren will inherit? What can you do to give them a promising future on this planet?

Those of us over 50 have a great many gifts and skills to contribute. We also have a responsibility to use them well. If you want to leave this kind of legacy, begin to consider what you want to offer and how you plan to demonstrate your values to others.

# Part
# Two

*Revivement Life Worksheets*

## Introduction

The following exercises have been developed based on my experiences with thousands of people in the workplace over the course of my career. These activities have been adapted to fit the needs of revivement, and I have identified what I believe would make life exciting and meaningful. I hope they take you to a new level of awareness and happiness.

These 15 exercises are designed to walk you through your revivement as you discover more about yourself and the life you want most. Although it is most helpful to do these exercises before you retire, they are also designed to be used if you are already retired.

Select the exercises based on what fits best for you. Write your results in the two-part "big-picture plan" at the end of all of the exercises. This will be your own tailor-made guide to refer to as you navigate your future.

If you are planning your revivement over the next 12 months, do one or more exercises per month. If you are planning your revivement over a six-month period, double up on the exercises per month. If you are at a different stage of life, pick goal dates to accomplish these activities and stick to them. Or, you can just do exercises that are meaningful to you.

You also might want to form a Mastermind Group or a Book Study Group where you can support each other in completing and activating these exercises.

If a question appears to have been asked in a previous exercise, please know that I have purposely repeated a few items in several different ways so that anyone who does not do some of the exercises can still benefit from the ones they answer.

I suggest you make copies of the blank exercise pages in the book to write on so that you can use the book over and over again to revise, change, or upgrade any of your initial ideas.

Enjoy your revivement journey!

# Exercise One

## Self-Exploration

*Check or fill in the blanks that are relevant to you.*

1. ☐ I am already in revivement
   ☐ I plan to revive in _____ (*month/year*)
   ☐ I never want to stop working
   ☐ I want to work at something new
   ☐ I want to continue working at my present profession

2. **What I understand about revivement is:**
   ☐ It is the end of my work life
   ☐ I will never be able work again because of my age
   ☐ I know ☐ don't know how I will spend my days
   ☐ I have a choice and can decide to work if I want to
   ☐ I can begin to do things on my bucket list
   What else _____

   _____

3. **My greatest fears about revivement are:**
   ☐ Getting old and frail
   ☐ Being bored
   ☐ Not knowing how to spend and manage my time
   ☐ Outliving my finances
   ☐ Missing co-workers

☐ Not knowing how to access new activities

☐ Not sure of what I want to do ☐

Other: _____

_____

4. **What I think my revivement will look like:**

☐ Sleeping late

☐ Reading

☐ Playing golf, tennis, swimming

☐ Going to the gym

☐ Working part-time

Add more here:

_____

_____

Whether you are planning your revivement or are already there, write a paragraph about what your life is like today and what it will be like in six months, after you incorporate new ways to enjoy revivement.

My Revivement life today

_____

_____

_____

_____

_____

My Revivement life in six months

_____

_____

_____

_____

_____

5. **What are you looking forward to when you revive?**
   *Check the boxes.*
   - ☐ Doing all the things I've always wanted to do
   - ☐ To get up when I want to each morning
   - ☐ Hobbies and activities on my bucket list
   - ☐ Starting an entrepreneurial venture
   - ☐ More time for family and friends
   - ☐ Playing more golf/tennis/ping pong

   Add more here:

   _____

   _____

6. **My attitude about revivement is:**
   - ☐ Good
   - ☐ Questionable
   - ☐ Fearful
   - ☐ Other

7. **What I want to get out of this book:**

☐ Direction/guidance

☐ Design for my path

☐ Know how I will spend my next years

☐ More:

_____

_____

_____

Now, make a list that essentially reacquaints you with yourself. Here are the basics to start with:

1. Jobs I've had that I enjoyed:

_____

_____

_____

2. Skills I've developed that I want to use:

_____

_____

_____

3. Wins/losses I experienced and what they taught me:

_____

_____

_____

4. Fears I have about my future:

_____

_____

_____

5.  Relationships that I want to grow:

_____

_____

_____

5. Relationships I want to let go of:

_____

_____

_____

6.  Hobbies I want to try:

_____

_____

_____

7. Goals I want to create:

_____

_____

_____

8. Spiritual beliefs I hold dear and want to explore further:

_____

_____

_____

9. Volunteer work I've done that I enjoyed:

_____

_____

_____

10. What else:

_____

_____

_____

_____

_____

_____

_____

_____

_____

_____

_____

_____

_____

## Exercise Two

### The First Six Months

This is the first day of the rest of your second half of life. You may decide to sleep in just for the fun of it, or you might decide to spring out of bed because you can't wait to start your new adventure. You choose!

Before we start designing your plan and see what decisions you want to make to guide you during your first six months of revivement, let's look at how Jack started his journey. Jack's story will give you an example of what these first days of revivement could look like.

*Jack looked at his options from the checklist below, and decided he would spend his first month traveling in Europe with his wife. Prior to his revivement party, he had a travel agent help him design their trip.*

*He took his first week of freedom to just relax, catch up on some things, and enjoy being home. Then on day eight, he and Sally boarded a plane and were off. Interesting, he thought, I don't have to worry about what's piling up on my desk while I'm gone anymore.*

*Jack and Sally thoroughly enjoyed their trip, but were ready to come home by day 29. Now the real test of revivement would begin.*

*Jack pulled out his Revivement Guide from this book. Since he followed the book and made his plan while he was still working, he knew his next steps. He began his revivement with a sense of excitement and peace.*

Of course, there are so many ways to start your journey. Do what works for you.

**Here are some questions to get you started:**

**1.** How do I want to spend the first six months of revival/ renewal after my years of working?

_____

_____

**a.** How much time do I want to just hangout and de-stress?

_____

**b.** How much time do I want to travel?

_____

**c.** How much time do I want to spend visiting family/friends?

_____

**d.** Do I just want to wing it, or do I want a plan?

_____

**e.** When do I want to begin activating my revivement plan?

_____

**f.** How much time do I want to allot every week for exercise?

_____

**g.** How much time do I want to spend reading the books I've always wanted to get around to reading?

_____

**h.** What else do I want to do?

_____

_____

## Exercise Three

### Dealing with Change and Loss

You know you will be reviving soon, or have already revived, and by reading this book you realize this will be a dramatic change for you. Chapter Three describes the stages people go through when a big transition occurs. You may want to reread that section before starting this exercise.

You may want to embrace the following process to help you adjust emotionally to the reality of the changes that occur naturally as you transition to the next stage of life. Understand that feeling emotional is a normal reaction to change, and you will get through it. Write your thoughts about each feeling below as you experience it. If you have already come through the experience, explore how it happened, as that may help bring closure.

Begin by choosing a context for your answers, whether it is retiring, losing your job because your company is downsizing, or another challenge that occurred.

Context: _____

**Denial** — *"This can't be happening to me."*
What do you understand is the reality of your new situation?

_____

_____

_____

**Anger** — *"Why is this happening? Who is to blame?"*
Who or what are/were you angry at?

_____

_____

_____

**Bargaining** — *"Make this not happen, and in return I will*
*do anything."*
What are your thoughts about? What would you be willing to
do to address this feeling?

_____

_____

_____

**Depression** —— *"I'm too sad to do anything."*
Do you really believe you are no longer in charge of changing
your situation? Why?

_____

_____

_____

**Acceptance** — *"I'm at peace with what happened."*
"I understand now, and I am ready to move forward."
What have you learned?

_____

_____

_____

## Exercise Four

### What I Never Want to Do Again

This is a fun exercise because you get to write down all of the things that you never want to do in your life again.

Examples:

1. I never want to have to get up before 7 am again.

2. I never want to work or hang out with negative people again.

3. I never want to do things that bore me again.

4. I never want to drive during commute hours again.

5. I never want to feel stressed about deadlines again.

Make your list. Get it all out of your system. Why? Because you're in charge of your future, and you get to choose what you do and don't want to do. List as many as 25 "I never want to's..." here. Don't stop at 25 if you have more than that!

1. _____

2. _____

3. _____

4. _____

5. _____

6. _____

7. _____

8. _____

9. _____

10. _____

11. _____

12. _____

13. _____

14. _____

15. _____

16. _____

17. _____

18. _____

19. _____

20. _____

21. _____

22. _____

23. _____

24. _____

25. _____

## Exercise Five

### Relationship with Self

Your mind believes everything you tell it. If you say you're good, it believes you are. If you say you're bad, it believes you are. It's time to eliminate negative and preconceived messages and empower your relationship with yourself. This activity will help you move beyond messaging that is not authentically you, and help you identify your true self at this stage of life.

Start by listing the internal messages that promote negative ideas about yourself. Then you are going to take each one and rewrite it into a positive message. Then you will look into your mirror, and with deep sincerity tell yourself that positive message. Bring it into your consciousness as if it already is true, because it actually is! Do this five times each day for the next two months. At that time assess your progress. Then do this activity more, until the positive messages are ingrained into your consciousness.

In the meantime, the second you hear your internal self giving you negative messages say "erase!" and replace them with positive messages. Reframing negative messages will take awareness. You'll need to be conscious of what you think. Your immediate self-corrections will override the negative messages. You might even notice after a while that you feel much better about yourself.

**1. List five things you think about that undermine you. Use the following ideas or any starters that will serve this purpose:**

"I'm not good at…

"I'll never fit in because…

_____

"I did such a dumb thing when…

_____

"I'll never look good in…

_____

"I'm just not smart enough to…

_____

**2. Now write the list over using the following stems:**

"I am good at…

_____

"I always fit in because…

_____

"I always learn from my mistakes. In this case I…

_____

"I always look good in…

_____

"I am smart about many things, including…

_____

Take each one of the positive items you wish to rerecord in your brain, look in the mirror and say them five times every day for a month. It may feel awkward or uncomfortable at first, but if you're in a private place (I used to lock myself in the bathroom) then it's just you, supporting yourself by making positive changes for yourself.

## Exercise Six

### Your Life Theme

We often follow paths throughout our lives that have similar themes. If we explore clues from childhood, young adulthood, and later years, we can often see a pattern that identifies this path and find information about who we are and where we might like to be in our future.

Example: One of my themes was about helping others. *In my internal stories as a young girl, I was always rescuing or saving or caring for someone. I can remember going to school on a bus and making up a story about being a nurse. Or, if someone was getting hurt, I would come to his or her rescue by tricking the assailant away from the victim. As a young person, I also volunteered. I read to a girl who had polio, who was in an iron lung, and I wrote letters for a blind older woman. When I was 18, I volunteered at a hospital. Without really knowing why, I desired to be of service. In my later years I continue to be involved in helping others by volunteering in several organizations. This theme has followed me in both the nonprofit and professional worlds, and added greatly to my desire to continue helping people. This desire to help has also translated into providing guidance and support in my work. It is the driving force behind this book. I want to share what I've learned with others about revivement.*

Another example:
*Throughout my life I always took on leadership roles, both professionally and as a volunteer. As I look back, at 19, while I was in college, I was president of my girls' club, on the student governing committee, and VP*

*of another group. I continued to take on leadership roles throughout my career as a manager, board member and president of professional and nonprofit organizations. It surprises me because I didn't grow up with an awareness that I would ever follow that path. But, there it is. So, if I was doing this exercise, I would think about how I would want to use my leadership skills going forward.*

There are other themes in my life that I can see by looking back. Each theme shows me an aspect of who I am today, and why what I do is purposeful for me.

You might want to try this activity to help you explore your next steps. Think of a stream of thoughts and activities that have followed you during your lifetime. Write a few paragraphs about what you've done from your younger years to today, and note the elements these activities have in common. Do you recognize a theme? As you are writing about one theme, you might remember others. List them separately so you can go back and explore them. Do this with each idea and let the activity paint a picture of yourself as you've grown into who you have become. The exercise below will get you started.

Once you finish your first theme, go back and mark the approximate dates, as well as what each activity has in common. Name each theme for easy reference. For example, I named my first theme "helping others" and my second theme "leadership."

**Theme One:**

1. What types of things did you find yourself involved in again and again when you were young? List them here:

_____

_____

_____

_____

_____

2. Do you connect with the same activities as an adult? List the ones you have continued.

_____

_____

_____

_____

3. What are some of the elements of those activities?

_____

_____

_____

_____

**4.** Are those activities relevant to you today?

_____

_____

_____

_____

_____

**5.** If yes, do you want to use those activities today?

_____

_____

_____

_____

**6.** How?

_____

_____

_____

_____

7. Do you see a pattern/theme?

_____

_____

_____

_____

_____

Name this theme:

_____

**Theme 2:**

1. What types of things did you find yourself involved in again and again when you were young? List them here:

_____

_____

_____

_____

_____

2. Do you connect with the same activities as an adult?
   List the ones you have continued.

   _____

   _____

   _____

   _____

   _____

3. What are some of the elements of those activities?

   _____

   _____

   _____

   _____

   _____

4. Are those activities relevant to you today?

   _____

   _____

   _____

   _____

   _____

5. If yes, do you want to use those activities today?

_____

_____

_____

_____

_____

6. How?

_____

_____

_____

_____

7. Do you see a pattern/theme?

_____

_____

_____

_____

_____

**Name this theme:**

_____

**Theme 3:**
1.  What types of things did you find yourself involved in again and again when you were young? List them here:

_____

_____

_____

_____

2.  Do you connect with the same activities as an adult? List the ones you have continued.

_____

_____

_____

3.  What are some of the elements of those activities?

_____

_____

_____

_____

4   Are those activities relevant to you today?

_____

_____

_____

_____

_____

5.  If yes, do you want to use those activities today?

_____

_____

_____

_____

_____

6.  How?

_____

_____

_____

_____

_____

7.  Do you see a pattern/theme? _____

Name this theme:

_____

# Exercise Seven

## Values Clarification

Your values drive your behavior. They are the silent forces behind many of your actions and decisions. They are why you behave, believe, and respond in certain ways. Your values impact the choices you make about how you live your life, interact with others, and move forward during challenging times. These essential components of yourself are intertwined with how you were socialized growing up. They are impacted by the decisions you made along the way to buy into or rebel against the social mores at the time. You can either accept and celebrate or change them. As always, you are at choice. They are reflections of who you are today.

Select ten of your most important values from this list by checking the boxes. Then prioritize them, with 'one' being of highest value. Understand that selecting the top ten does not mean you don't have other respected values on the list. You are welcome to choose and prioritize them all. Just for the sake of this exercise, I'm asking you to select ten to give you something to start with.

| | | | |
|---|---|---|---|
| ☐ | Acceptance | ☐ | Creativity |
| ☐ | Adventure | ☐ | Empathy |
| ☐ | Appreciation | ☐ | Exercise |
| ☐ | Caring | ☐ | Fairness |
| ☐ | Choice | ☐ | Family |
| ☐ | Communication | ☐ | Flexibility |
| ☐ | Compassion | ☐ | Freedom |

- [ ] Friendships
- [ ] Fun
- [ ] Health/Wellness
- [ ] Joy
- [ ] Justice
- [ ] Honesty
- [ ] Humor
- [ ] Independence
- [ ] Integrity
- [ ] Knowledge
- [ ] Learning
- [ ] Love
- [ ] Money
- [ ] Peace

- [ ] Popularity
- [ ] Power
- [ ] Purpose
- [ ] Reason
- [ ] Relationships
- [ ] Respect
- [ ] Responsibility
- [ ] Safety
- [ ] Self-Esteem
- [ ] Spirituality
- [ ] Stability
- [ ] Success
- [ ] Wisdom

Please add other values that have meaning to you, and include them in your prioritized list.

Next, write each of the ten values and a sentence or two about what that value means to you.

1.

2.

3.

4.

5.

**6.**

**7.**

**8.**

**9.**

**10.**

You can use this list for the Celebrating Your 100th Birthday
in Exercise Eight. You can also take your values forward to
use in Exercise Nine for Developing Your Purpose.

## Exercise Eight

### Celebrating Your Life on Your 100th Birthday

Let's say you have just turned 100, and people have gathered to celebrate this auspicious day with you. You know you have accumulated wisdom, knowledge, and beliefs that you want to share with your friends and family. You've had a vision of your life that has unfolded, and you feel you've purposefully led your life to become the person you are today. You have written a speech, designed visual aids to bring impact to your talk, and have practiced it over and over. On this day, you will stand upon the stage and offer the best of who you are as you share your wisdom and lessons about life, as well as your hopes and dreams for those who follow you.

You want to be remembered for who you are and what you've accomplished. You want to share your values, beliefs and other actions that have made your time on this planet meaningful, that have made you, you.

Before this special day can happen, we need to go back one year to when you turned 99. This is when you made up your mind to prepare for your 100th birthday by writing and practicing the thoughts you plan to share. This activity is a deep and thoughtful project, so you decide to give time to it every day for the next few months to write and rehearse so you'll be ready. Of course, you may not need that long.

Your purpose is to guide and educate—to leave this information as part of your legacy. You might even decide, once your speech is completed, to print booklets of your talk with photos so your family and friends can take away the value you have produced.

No matter your age today, with these instructions in mind, begin your personal legacy writing as if you were 100. Experience this exercise as a living document. Know you can come back to this exercise as your thoughts continue to evolve. You can use this writing to help determine how you want to use the rest of your life, and you can make changes to it along the way.

**Instructions:**

Here are a few ways to get you started. Get a notebook that you dedicate to this project. Write your name and "My Life" on the cover. Write in a private, quiet space that allows you to think. You can also go for a walk and record your thoughts on your phone or a small tape recorder.

Just allow your ideas to flow. Don't criticize them, fix them, or share them. At this point, you need to keep this information to yourself so it isn't changed by outside influences. At the same time, without sharing what you write, you can ask people close to you to describe how they see you.

Another way to begin is to make a list of your values first (using Exercise Seven), and then write with these values in mind.

# Guidelines

Start your speech design by using this format to help you think of a few of the ideas that you want to use in your talk. Then use your special booklet to advance your ideas and complete your talk. Take your time to write this special talk. Once you feel satisfied that you've accomplished this task, ask a few close and trusted friends or family members to listen to your talk and give you constructive feedback. All professional speakers do this to ensure their performance will be the best it can be.

## I. Preparation

### Step One
Write an opening for your talk—a short paragraph—that will grab your audience's attention.

### Step Two
Jot down three to five main ideas you want to cover.

### Step Three
Write two to three sentences under each main idea that describes what you want to say. You can write more details later.

### Step Four
List three to five stories you want to fit into your talk that you feel are relevant to your message, entertaining and informative for your listeners, and underscore the points you want to make.

### Step Five
Write a closing that wraps up your talk, and what you hope your listeners will take away from this special event.

## II. Practice

Practice is an essential process that helps us perfect our talks. If you are not used to speaking in front of groups, get a speech coach. And, practice, practice, practice.

## III. Visual Aids

Have someone help you put together a video or PowerPoint that adds meaning to your talk.

**Notes:**

# Exercise Nine

## Who Are You? — A Play

**Instructions:** Read the following exercise and questions fully before you start writing. Let the ideas germinate in your mind. Then respond to the questions.

The play opens with you sitting on the couch in a state of confusion. You are newly reviving and wondering, "Oh my, now what?"

The doorbell rings. You open the door and different parts of you come to visit. Each has a request.

First your thinking self walks through the door. "What do you want to do with me now? I'm a marvelous and intelligent mind that has helped you think through your days, nights, ups, and downs. We've been through a lot together. Now what?"

The bell rings again. In walks your creativity. "What innovations, inspirations, and ideas do we want to create to move you forward? How do you want to use me?"

One by one, each of your attributes—skills, talents, feelings, desires— come through the door with the same words: "Use me, please. I'm here for you."

All these parts of yourself may seem overwhelming. "Okay, okay," you say. "Slow down. It's hard for me to take this in all at once." You pick one area to start. Let's say, as an example, it's your creativity. "Well," you say, "I've always wanted to feel clay in my hands and shape it into something magnificent. While I might not make something magnificent at first, I won't know until I try. Maybe I'll take a class in sculpting." You look up potential classes, check your schedule, and register. You start the class with trepidation but realize once you're there that you enjoy it. You say to yourself, "I think I'll continue this for a while." Congratulations! One part of the play is written.

As you investigate the puzzle that is you, you begin to see other options. You sit there, astonished that you are made up of all of these pieces. This never occurred to you before. Suddenly, the recognition of who you are lifts your spirit and you are ready to begin anew.

Based on who you are, and your interests and skills, you might say, "I like working with numbers, so I can help people with their taxes." "I can use my athletic skills to teach kids soccer." "Maybe I can use my creativity to decorate someone's home." The list goes on and on as you match your attributes with activities you would enjoy. As you put your plan together, how you will spend your time during the next few years becomes clear. You'll add in your social connections, family, spiritual life, volunteer activities, leisure, and other priorities. Once you have some structure that will help put your life in balance, you can choose how you want to proceed. Life is good!

The play is an ongoing hit. Applause! Applause!

What follows is a four-part exercise. Don't feel you need to do it all at once. You can do one or two parts at a time.

In Part One, you will identify words that describe parts of you.
In Part Two, you will retrieve your ideas.
In Part Three, you will write down how you feel when using these parts of yourself.
In Part Four, how you want to use your attributes and skills.

## Part One

Find a comfortable spot where you can relax and not be interrupted. You can start with just one attribute, or do a few at once. I suggest picking five from the list on page 211 to begin, and create a use for each one. You can imagine these uses, or you can record them and play them back to yourself.

Start by answering the following questions:
What attributes do you want to use to move you forward?

What skills do you want to use to move you forward?

Here are some examples of ideas to choose from. Make the list yours by adding your own:

- ☐ Actor
- ☐ Artistic
- ☐ Athletic
- ☐ Conscientious
- ☐ Creative
- ☐ Dependable
- ☐ Design
- ☐ Entrepreneurial
- ☐ Focus
- ☐ Gets the job done
- ☐ Handy/good at fixing things
- ☐ Helps others
- ☐ Idea person
- ☐ Integrity
- ☐ Internal problem-solver
- ☐ Learning
- ☐ Listener
- ☐ Math
- ☐ Mechanical fixer
- ☐ Meditation
- ☐ Multi-tasker
- ☐ Musician
- ☐ Music lover
- ☐ Nature lover
- ☐ Outgoing
- ☐ People skills
- ☐ Personal skills
- ☐ Public speaking
- ☐ Reader
- ☐ Responsible
- ☐ Social
- ☐ Solution-oriented
- ☐ Speaker
- ☐ Strong people skills
- ☐ Thinking/cognitive skills
- ☐ Travel
- ☐ Words
- ☐ Writing
- ☐ Yoga

## Part Two

When each part of you asks: "What do you want to do with me now?" that means you want to take action.

A good way to retrieve your ideas is to write down anything that comes to mind. Make a wish list of at least 25 activities and ideas that you might like to incorporate in your life, in which you can use your skills and attributes. Use the list on page 211. They can be something you already do or a totally new experience. Examples include learning to swim or play the piano, joining a bowling team, going on a safari, taking an oil painting class, learning a new profession or skill. Don't be constrained by whether you will or will not actually do them. Just write them all down here.

This activity requires pushing aside your inner critic, that part of you that feels insecure, that thinks maybe your ideas aren't good enough. The inner critic blocks the flow of creativity. So we tell the critic to go away for now, to give ourselves a chance to explore. When we hear our critics trying to sneak back in to our thoughts, we put them aside.

Here is an example of how to use this exercise. I'm selecting the word 'solution-oriented' from the list.

*Imagine you are sitting in your living room and the doorbell rings. When you open the door it's your solution-oriented self, who says, "I'm a marvelous problem-solver. We've been through a lot together. What do you want to do with me now? How do you want to use me?"*

*You are astonished. You sit back down and pause, then realize what it is you'd like to do with your problem-solving skill. "I always wanted to help solve environmental issues," you answer with some concern, as this seems like a monumental undertaking. You put this on your wish list and again answer the doorbell.*

*Another attribute walks in. One by one, all your attributes, some hidden, some familiar, walk in and ask, "How do you want to use me?"*

*After each one, you sit back down and pause, then realize what it is you'd like to do with each attribute, and write your answers on your wish list.*

When you are complete with this portion of the exercise, continue on with the writing section that follows. Or, if you need to stop for a while, decide when you will return to parts three and four.

**Part Three**

One by one, expand the 25 things on your wish list. Complete the exercise below by using "feeling" words: good, alive, proud, happy, engaged, smart, useful, energetic, etc.

Continue expanding these activities until you've completed all 25 activities on your wish list. Then prioritize them, starting with what excites you the most.

Idea 1: When I'm doing

    I feel

Idea 2: When I'm doing

    I feel

Idea 3: When I'm doing

  I feel

Idea 4: When I'm doing

  I feel

Idea 5: When I'm doing

  I feel

Idea 6: When I'm doing

  I feel

Idea 7: When I'm doing

  I feel

Idea 8: When I'm doing

  I feel

Idea 9 When I'm doing

  I feel

Idea 10: When I'm doing

  I feel

Idea 11: When I'm doing

    I feel

Idea 12: When I'm doing

    I feel

Idea 13: When I'm doing

    I feel

Idea 14: When I'm doing

    I feel

Idea 15: When I'm doing

    I feel

sIdea 16: When I'm doing

    I feel

Idea 17: When I'm doing

    I feel

Idea 18: When I'm doing

    I feel

Idea 19: When I'm doing

I feel

Idea 20: When I'm doing

I feel

Idea 21: When I'm doing

I feel

Idea 22: When I'm doing

I feel

Idea 23: When I'm doing

I feel

Idea 24: When I'm doing

I feel

Idea 25: When I'm doing

I feel

**Part Four**

Think about the end result you want to achieve with the attributes you wrote down in the previous exercises. Do you want to create products, services, experiences? Do you want to help others? Do you just want to enjoy them? Write down your answers here:

What else do you want to create to support you in having a fulfilling revivement?

1.

2.

3.

4.

5.

Now prioritize your ideas in the order of what excites you the most.

1.


2.


3.


4.


5.

When you are satisfied with your top five ideas, begin to make an action plan—to actually enjoy them. Give yourself "deadlines" to actually start doing them.

What do you want to create to move you forward?

Action                                                    Begin

# Exercise Ten

## Developing Your Purpose

Writing down the answers to the questions below helps you think by putting hand and mind together to formulate ideas. Identify who you are and how you wish to use yourself in the world. Let the content come from what's inside you. Think about what you enjoy, how it can help others, and what you want to accomplish by using who you are for the greater good. Your personal purpose will evolve from your thinking and writing. You will experience profound satisfaction as you fulfill your personal mission (the next activity), for it represents your contribution to the world.

**Purpose Discovery**

Who am I?

What are some of the patterns that have run through my life?

What motivated me to overcome challenges?

What did I dream about being when I was young?


What type of people have I always enjoyed being around?


What things always gave me pleasure?


What activities did I hate?


What activities were so engrossing that they made the day fly by?

221

What kinds of activities was I drawn to again and again?

What have I done in my spare time?

What kinds of movies, books, and lectures am I drawn to?

What other aspects of me do I want to include here?

Now review your answers and think deeply how they direct you to your personal purpose. Select elements from your answers that seem to connect into a purpose pattern, and form a purpose statement from them.

Examples:

I want to be involved in conservation.

I want to help people live healthier lives.

I want to educate others on the benefits of peace.

Write your ideas below, or you can move on to the next exercise that continues this thinking and fold it into a personal mission statement (the next exercise).

# Exercise Eleven

## Developing Your Mission Statement

This exercise is to help you develop your personal mission statement. Your personal mission will guide your decisions, activities, and life path, and help you develop a fulfilling future aligned with your values and desires.

By using your purpose statement from the previous exercise, and answering the questions below, you will identify how you wish to use yourself in the world. The answers come from what's inside of you. Think about what you enjoy, how it can help others, and what you want to accomplish by using who you are and your skills for the greater good. This exercise takes time and deep thought. Combine your thoughts into a mission statement. Use the examples below.

**Fill in the blanks:**

1. What do I do well?

2. What are my ten highest values?

3.What are my skills, talents, capabilities?

4.How do I want to use them?

5.How do I want to use my skills for the greater good, to help others, the environment, and the world?

The following ideas are samples of mission statements to use as a guide. Of course, your end result should be unique to you.

"My mission is to make a difference in the lives of others by sharing my knowledge, life experiences, lessons, and guidance to help them achieve their personal goals."

"My mission is to use my love of nature and the environment to spearhead sustainable programs that preserve and renew the lands of the world."

"My mission is to help people overcome their fears and negative internal messages so they can live confident lives."

"My mission is to help children get the education they need to be productive and happy citizens."

"My mission is to use my concern about people who do not have enough food for nourishment by volunteering in food distribution centers."

"My mission is to use the skills I acquired during my work years to help retired entrepreneurs achieve success in their new business."

"My mission is to help families heal and support each other, starting with my own."

Use this space to complete the development of your mission statement.

# Exercise 12

## Activities and Hobbies to Enjoy

Make a list of 25 activities and hobbies you have liked in the past and those you have always wanted to try. Include leisure, volunteering, work, or any category of activity that you want to try. Here are some ideas to choose from, but don't hesitate to come up with your own. Check all that interest you.

- ☐ Birding
- ☐ Boating
- ☐ Book Clubs
- ☐ Bow & Arrow Target Practice
- ☐ Building Model Ships
- ☐ Café Clubs
- ☐ Card Games
- ☐ Choirs
- ☐ Cooking Clubs or Classes
- ☐ Dancing
- ☐ Decorating
- ☐ Gardening
- ☐ Golf

- ☐ Hiking/walking
- ☐ Lectures
- ☐ Music performances
- ☐ Movies
- ☐ Painting
- ☐ Photography
- ☐ Plays
- ☐ Sailing
- ☐ Sculpting
- ☐ Swimming
- ☐ Tennis
- ☐ Travel

Let's say your three priorities are to join a choir, to mentor teenagers, and to work at your present profession part-time. Your next step is to list the priority, strategy to achieve the priority, tactics that support the strategy, and finally the actions you are going to take.

As an example, using the word "my" to own this plan, write down:

1. My first priority is to join a choir.

2. Strategy: Investigate several community and religious choirs.

3. Tactics with specific target dates:
   • Call three to five choir organizers and ask what type of music they sing, if they perform, where and when they perform, and if you can sit in on their next rehearsal and listen. Make the calls by_____ date.

   • Attend rehearsals and listen to hear if the music fits your style by _____date.

4. Action: Choose one choir to join. Join!

5. Show up for practice.

6. Participate in shows.

Fit this activity into the related heading below. Do this with the other activities.

Periodically review your list to expand and alter it as your interests evolve. You might decide to put them in a new order or add and subtract from your list. When you've done your first three, then choose your next three activities to explore.

Use the word "my" to own this plan and write down:
1. My first priority is to:

2. My strategy is:

3. My tactics with specific target dates are:

4. Action:

5. Show up at:

6. Participate in:

# Exercise 13

## Planning as a Couple

Please read the pages in the book in Chapter Five about how Nat and Nancy planned their retirement together. Use their list to support your process.

Set up a time to meet together to talk about how you will revive as a couple. Find a quiet space where you won't be interrupted and will be able to focus on each other.

Decide together the length and dates of your first and future meetings. I suggest starting with two-hour segments, but space out the timing of each segment to keep yourselves from burning out.

Make sure you have pen and paper available to take notes. At the end of each meeting, share your notes to make sure you both understand.

If both of you are taking notes, review each other's notes. Acknowledge the areas you agreed upon, and talk about areas you understand differently.

Before you begin, it's important to decide how you will communicate and listen to each other, so make the following agreements by reading them out loud:

1. When we communicate I will listen quietly and not interrupt or make you wrong.

2. I will respond to your comments caringly and tell you my concerns.

3. We will speak the truth in a kind and respectful manner.

4. I understand that you are an individual and try to see things from your perspective.

5. When we don't agree, we will discuss the issue in an adult, non-judgmental manner.

6. I will be open to the fact that some of your needs are different from mine.

7. I will be supportive of you achieving what you want.

8. I am open to planning how we will spend time together as a couple.

9. When we finish a meeting, we will summarize what we heard and plan our next meeting.

10. We'll thank each other for the gift of planning our revivement together, and give each other a big hug.

In your meeting, list the areas that are important to both of you. Make a list, a guide, together; it must be flexible. You may want to include the following items and add more of your own:

1. How much time will we spend together as a couple?

2. How much time will we spend doing our own thing?

3. What things do we enjoy in common?

4. Of those activities, what should we plan to do together?

5. Where do we want to live? Do we want to keep our present home or move?

6. How will we share our living space?

7. Do we want to travel? How often? Where?

8. Who will do the cooking, buy the food, clean the house?

9. In what ways will we acknowledge each other?

10. How will we agree to disagree?

Write more ideas that are important to you.

## Exercise 14

### Planning When You're Single

You can choose to do this exercise by yourself, or find another person or friend in revivement to brainstorm with:

1. How do I plan to get out into the world to enjoy who I am and fully experience life?

   - [ ] Call friends
   - [ ] Travel with friends, groups or by myself
   - [ ] Attend events
   - [ ] Take classes
   - [ ] Explore avenues of interest
   - [ ] Find part-time work
   - [ ] Other

2. What will I do to make sure I socialize and don't become isolated?

   - [ ] Join a few organizations that meet weekly or monthly
   - [ ] Volunteer at a nonprofit that requires me to show up on a schedule
   - [ ] Find a book club to discuss what I'm reading
   - [ ] Get involved in my community
   - [ ] Start a project that requires others' involvement
   - [ ] Other

3. What will stimulate me to feel rewarded from the inside out?

&#9744; Get focused on my purpose and mission
&#9744; Meet with others to carry my mission forward
&#9744; Use my skills to provide services
&#9744; Other

4. What and when will I do the items on my bucket list?
*(write your bucket list and some dates here)*

5. How often do I want to enjoy my alone time?

6. Would I like to find a life partner?

7. Would I like someone to share my home?

If you answer yes to 6 and/or 7, it is important to define the parameters that make each relationship a success. So ask yourself:

1. What qualities and attributes does that person need to have?

2. What values does the person need to have?

3. What behaviors and other habits will support a successful time together?

4. How do I want to structure arrangements to share
a home with someone?

5. How will I find the right person as a partner or to share my
home with?

6. Write more ideas here.

# Exercise 15

## Leaving a Legacy

Below are questions from my granddaughters' school projects that I answered in Chapter Six. This space is for your answers.

Use the questions that fit for you. Write your answers as if you are telling someone younger what you believe and how you have lived your life. As a bonus, decide how you want to share your list. You can choose to give it to those you love, those you mentor or anyone you feel will benefit from your list.

Write your answers to the questions below:

1) What career advice can you give me?

2) What advice about life can you share with me?

3) What is the best way to deal with disappointment?

4) What can you tell me about dealing with low self-esteem?

5) Who do you suggest as people to admire?

6) When is the most important time in life?

7) What advice would you give a young adult who is unsure
   of a direction?

8) What qualities make a person successful in life?

9) What qualities make a person a good person?

10) Are there any absolute or objective standards of right and wrong? If so, what are they?

11) Overall, what advice would you give to me about life? How I should live—my future, career, investments, technology, national politics, global politics, marriage and family?

**12)** How would you define happiness?

**13)** At this point, what is the highest priority of your life?

**14)** If someone asked you to explain your philosophy of life (the ideals you live by), what would you say? What reasons would you give to justify your answer?

**15)** What is your view concerning the existence of God or the nature of ultimate reality? What reasons would you give to justify your answer?

**16)** In your view, what are the most basic or fundamental human problems?

**17)** Is there a solution to the most basic human problems? If so, what is it?

**18)** What qualities do you think best suit a mentor?

**19)** What question do you most wish you could answer in your life?

## Wrap Up One

### MY REVIVEMENT SUMMARY

Name_____ Start Date _____

Congratulations on working through the exercises to develop your plan! Now put the information from each exercise into this final document so you can see the total picture of how you want to enjoy your revivement.

Fill in the following blank areas from each exercise.

Exercise One—*Self-Exploration*
Date Completed: _____

**1.** During my second half of life, I want to:

**2.** What I want to get out of this book:

Exercise Two—*The First Six Months*
Date Completed: _____

Write a paragraph describing how you want to live in revivement during the first six months after you retire.

Exercise Three—*Dealing with Change and Loss*
Date Completed: _____

**1.** The stage I'm in now is:

**2.** Other stages I might still need to deal with are:

**3.** What it will take for me to accept my feelings of loss:

Exercise Four—*What I Never Want to Do Again:*
Date Completed: _____
List your top ten here.




Exercise Five—*Relationship with Self*
Date Completed: _____

List the positive messages you are integrating into your
everyday existence. Keep adding to this list as you introduce
yourself to new messages.

Exercise Six—*Life Theme*
Date Completed: _____

List your life themes. Take each one and write a short paragraph to concisely depict the path you've taken.

Exercise Seven—*Values Clarification*
Date Completed: _____

List your top ten here, knowing you have a longer list you can reference in the pages of this document.

Exercise Eight—Celebrating Your Life on Your 100th Birthday
Date Completed: _____

List the main three to five points you want to make sure to share in your talk.

Exercise Nine—*Who Are You: A Play*
Date Completed: _____

List the different aspects of you and how you will use them as you approach new chapters in your life. For instance, your thinking self, creative self, feeling self, playful self, serious self, etc.

Exercise Ten—*Develop Your Purpose*
Date Completed: _____

What is your purpose?

Exercise Eleven—*Develop Your Mission Statement*
Date Completed: _____

What is your mission, and how do you plan to activate it in the world?

Exercise Twelve—*Activities and Hobbies to Enjoy*
Date Completed: _____

What are your top ten favorite activities? After you list them, place a date by when you are going to invite each one into your life. If you are already involved in one or more of these activities, just check them off your list.

Exercise Thirteen—*Couple Exercise*
Date Completed: _____

What agreements have you made?

Exercise Fourteen—Single Exercise
Date Completed: _____

How are you going to interact in the world?

Exercise Fifteen—*Leaving a Legacy*
Date Completed: _____

Who will receive your legacy? When will you gift it to them?

Now transfer the core of your Revivement Summary to your Master Plan.

Once you've completed the exercises and your plan, put a few dates on your calendar to revisit what you've written and see if you need to make any changes.

They should be in three-month increments. At some point, you may feel a need to do more thinking, acting and being, and you can come back and do the exercises over and update your plan.

## Wrap Up Two

### MASTER PLAN

Name _____

Date_____

Design the life you want below by using the elements of an integrated life. Respond to each section to show how you plan to activate your desires, ideas and plans into your life.

One—*Purpose*
Idea:


Goals:


How to integrate:

What involvement looks like:

Two—*Work*
Idea:

Goals:

How to integrate:

What involvement looks like

Three—*Relationships*
Idea:


Goals:


How to integrate:


What involvement looks like:


Four—*Ongoing Learning*
Idea:

Goals:


How to integrate:


What involvement looks like:


Five—*Health/Wellness*
Idea:


Goals:


How to integrate:

What involvement looks like:

Six—*Lifestyle*
Idea:

Goals:

How to integrate:

What involvement looks like:

Seven—*Volunteerism*
Idea:

Goals:

How to integrate:

What involvement looks like:

Eight—*Spirit*
Idea:

Goals:


How to integrate:


What involvement looks like:


Nine—*Leisure*
Idea:


Goals:


How to integrate:

What involvement looks like:


Ten—*Legacy*
Idea:


Goals:


How to integrate:


What involvement looks like:

Eleven—*Finance*
Idea:

Goals:

How to integrate:

What involvement looks like:

# Conclusion

This book is designed to be a doorway to your revivement. You now understand that the new model called revivement is not about endings, but about beginnings, becomings, and balance.

Remember all the people you've read about who are over 50 and having a great second half of life. I hope you learned from their struggles and wins so you will be eager to design the way you can make your own life work for you.

I hope the information here guided your thinking, motivated your desire for more, and enticed you to try new things. You are absolutely worth this investment.

Since life is complex, we all need guidance to be able to open doors within us that will enable us to find peace and happiness. Our attitude has an enormous impact on our lives. Sometimes just knowing that we ourselves are the source of the fountains of our inner youth helps. Remember, the body may age, but youth is in the mind.

Many of us have looked through our personal windows of change—sometimes with fear. Isn't it great to know that going through change is really about growth, not about someone or something beating us down? Because when we truly accept the challenge of change and overcome adversity, we become more of our very best selves.

Outside your door is a garden where you literally can smell the roses. But, remember, rose bushes have thorns that remind us to be careful how we handle our relationships, how we make decisions, and how we take care of ourselves. We learn how to enjoy the roses and pick them without hurting ourselves or anyone else. Change is the force that has shaken us out of our comfort areas to give us the opportunity to stand tall. We haven't necessarily been comfortable going through the many changes in our lives, but we have reached the other side of the changes, and should feel proud that we have grown from our experiences.

By designing your Master Plan, you have given yourself a great gift. Now you have a flexible guide to take you through those uncomfortable days that inevitably occur when you begin, or are in the middle of, your revivement. You'll know what you want and how to make it work. Happiness and satisfaction will fill your active days, and you'll be grateful for this new stage of life.

Finally, because you've accrued experience, skills, ideas, personal growth, and so much more during your life, you have the opportunity to use all of that to fulfill your personal purpose and mission. Fulfilling your purpose and mission will not only bring meaning to your life, it will be the legacy you leave when you complete your journey on earth.

You are now a model for other revivers. You have again changed the world. I salute your journey and am excited about your future.

# Bibliography

Barrow, Georgia M., and Smith, Patricia A., *Ageing, Ageism and Society*, West Publishing Co., May 1980

Buettner, Dan, *The Blue Zones*, National Geographic Society, 2012

Buettner, Dan, *The Blue Zone Solution*, National Geographic Society, 2015

Cruikshank, Margaret, *Learning to be Old: Gender, Culture, and Aging*, Rowman & Littlefield Publishers, Inc., Feb 14, 2013

Csikszentmihalyi, Mihaly, *Flow: The Psychology of Optimal Experience*, HarperCollins Publishers, July 1, 2008

Csikszentmihalyi, Mihaly, Creativity: *Flow and the Psychology of Discovery and Invention*, HarperCollins Publishers, Aug 6, 2013

Doidge, Norman, *The Brain That Changes Itself: Stories of Personal Triumph from the Frontiers of Brain Science*, Penguin Books, Dec 18, 2007

Donkin , Richard, *The History of Work*, Palgrave Macmillan, June 15, 2010

Dychtwald Ph.D, Ken with Daniel J. Kadlec, *The Power Years: A User's Guide to the Rest of Your Life*, John Wiley & Sons, Inc., September 1, 2005

Dychtwald Ph.D, Ken with Daniel J. Kadlec, *With Purpose: Redefining Money, Family, Work, Retirement and Success*, HarperCollins Publishers, October 6, 2009

Gullette, Margaret Morganroth, *AgeWise: Fighting the New Ageism in America*, University of Chicago Press, October 21, 2013

Junger, Sebastian, *Tribe: On Homecoming and Belonging*, Twelve, May 24, 2016

Merzenich PhD, Dr. Michael, *Soft-Wired: How the New Science of Brain Plasticity Can Change Your Life*, Parnassus Pubishing, LLC, Oct 14, 2013

Putnam, Robert D., *Bowling Alone: The Collapse and Revival of American Community*, Simon and Schuster, Aug 7, 2001

Shenk, David, *The Genius in All of Us: Why Everything You've Been Told About Genetics, Talent, and IQ Is Wrong*, Anchor Books, Random House, March 9, 2010

Thich Nhat Hanh, *Work: How to Find Joy and Meaning in Each Hour of the Day*, Penquin Randam House Publishers, Nov 8, 2008

Traynor, Barbara M., *Second Career Volunteer*, AuthorHouse, April 25, 2012

Ulrich, Dave and Ulrich, Wendy, *The Why of Work*, McGraw Hill, June 18, 2010

Wrisley, Bruce, *The Senior Homeowner's Housing Dilemma-Stay or Move?*, Bruce M. Wrisley, April 10, 2011

## About Gloria Dunn-Violin, Author

I've been fortunate to work at what I love to do to help people have their best life possible. I'm presently in my third career as a professional speaker, workshop leader and author, focused on helping pre- and present retirees plan a meaningful and fulfilling second half of life. I also advise corporations and business services on how to prepare their employees and clients with meaningful advice about retirement and aging.

For 25 years I provided services in training, coaching, and consulting in the field of Organizational Development and Behavior, and was a professional speaker through my own business: Wiser Ways to Work. During the preceding 10 years, I enjoyed my work as an award-winning public relations professional. I've written a book, *From Making a Living to Having a Life,* and many articles for newspapers and magazines, and hosted a Cable TV interview talk show with business professionals. I'm an active member of my community and the Rotary Club of Novato.

Visit me at: www.havingalifenow.com

# Index

Made in the USA
Middletown, DE
10 February 2020